PRAISE FOR *SUNBURNT COUNTRY, SWEEPING PAINS*

"Graham Joseph Hill is well-known as a scholar and an author who conveys the sound of the field. Many of his writings have focused on reflecting the voices of ethnic minorities, women, and marginal people in Christian ministry. Migration is one of the essential phenomena in missionary works. However, the traditional mainstream society does not understand the difficulties of immigrants. I recommend this book to pastors and missionaries amid a changing society."

—Timothy Hyun Mo Lee, Korea Baptist Theological Seminary

"*Sunburnt Country, Sweeping Pains* is an essential and honest look at the challenges that Asian Australian women have faced (and still face) as ministers of the gospel. It is a timely study for the church to examine in this rising season of justice that God is sweeping worldwide. May God use this book to bring about healing, redemption, and much-needed change for our sisters in ministry."

—Eddie Byun, Talbot School of Theology

"This is a timely book that spotlights the under-recognized contribution of Asian Australian women to Australia's increasingly diverse churches. Asian Australian women are uniquely gifted to create and facilitate third spaces and disciple and minister to people from third cultures. This book is essential for church ministers who wish to deeply embrace and empower their diverse congregations beyond mere representation."

—Enqi Weng, Deakin University

"This stimulating, accessible, and revealing book . . . makes visible the lived realities and the discrimination that migrant Asian women experience within society and the church. It shares their powerful and faith-filled efforts to foster a change that rests on values of equality, dignity, and justice within the church. This book enables the reader to appreciate and critically analyze the intersections of gender, ethnicity, and religion."

—MONICA JYOTSNA MELANCHTHON, Pilgrim Theological College, University of Divinity

"If you think that this book is a niche, think again! Graham Joseph Hill and Jessie Giyou Kim's research is timely and specific to Australian Christianity yet no less urgent and relevant to the rest of the church striving to be one new humanity in Christ in a diverse and globalized world. *Sunburnt Country, Sweeping Pains* is a unique and much-needed resource!"

—AHMI LEE, Fuller Theological Seminary

"*Sunburnt Country, Sweeping Pains* is a profoundly moving, biblically based, and excellent book on Asian Australian women's experiences of inequality, racism, sexism, and stereotypes well as joy and fulfillment in ministry and mission. It includes thirty-six constructive suggestions for dealing with such racism, sexism, and inequality. Highly recommended as essential reading!"

—SIANG-YANG TAN, Fuller Theological Seminary

"This pioneering book showcases the leadership and ministry of Asian Australian women and explores discrimination and barriers they face. Using an intersectional approach that includes race, gender, class, and migration, this book contributes to our understanding of the changing face of world Christianity. I highly recommend it."

—KWOK PUI-LAN, Candler School of Theology, Emory University

"This book breaks down the wall of orientalism in Australian society and the white male-dominated theological field. It contributes to true reconciliation in Christ between the host and the guest, enabling them to overcome the social gap. For the migrant and the diaspora generation living through the twenty-first-century pandemic, this book tills the earth to plant new seeds and let the marginalized voices echo."

—HANNA HYUN, Juan International University

"This is such necessary research capturing the lived experience and contributions of Asian Australian women in ministry! I grieved yet cheered and remained hopeful as I read experiences that echoed mine. I feel seen! This resource will challenge leaders of churches to make much-needed institutional change. Let's amplify voices from the margins and create spaces for their flourishing."

—CHARLENE DELOS SANTOS, Multicultural 2nd Gen Coordinator, Baptist Union of Victoria, Australia

"Hill and Kim believe that Asian Australian Christian women, in particular, are some of the good Samaritans. They can bring deep healing and hope to the dying churches in their country. . . . It remains to be seen whether white male-dominated churches in Australia (and America) will take their cues from Jesus and put their trust in those good Samaritans that they have typically marginalized and oppressed. I agree with the authors that failing to do so will be fatal."

—KEN FONG, former Senior Pastor, Evergreen Baptist Church of Los Angeles

"*Sunburnt Country, Sweeping Pains* initiates a long-overdue acknowledgement of the contributions of Asian women in the global church, with statistics and Scripture to back it up! . . . Graham Joseph Hill and Jessie Giyou Kim invite the global church to understand that the church's witness and effectiveness are enriched when they encourage and release Asian women in Australia and beyond to live into the fullness of how God has created them to be."

—ANN CHOW, Owner, Ann Chow Event and Project Management

"Hill and Kim's work challenges the church to work together by embracing our diversity. Graham's rare combination of academic brilliance, high level of self-awareness, and deep-rooted empathetic nature means that he can gift us with his wisdom on how we can listen to all voices as we move forward as a church. . . . I would recommend this book for all of us who strive to honor Christ with our lives."

—MELISSA RAMOO, Physiotherapist and Student of Ministry, Morling College

Sunburnt Country, Sweeping Pains

EDITORIAL TEAM

Editor in Chief

Graham Joseph Hill

Editorial Board

Darrell Jackson
Darren Cronshaw
Garry Deverell
Gina A. Zurlo
Grace Ji-Sun Kim
Graham Joseph Hill

Sunburnt Country, Sweeping Pains

The Experiences of Asian Australian Women
in Ministry and Mission

GRAHAM JOSEPH HILL

Forewords by
Grace Lung and Hanna Hyun

Afterword by
Grace Ji-Sun Kim

FAITH AND JUSTICE IN THESE LANDS
NOW CALLED AUSTRALIA

WIPF & STOCK · Eugene, Oregon

SUNBURNT COUNTRY, SWEEPING PAINS
The Experiences of Asian Australian Women in Ministry and Mission

Copyright © 2022 Graham Joseph Hill. All rights reserved. Except for brief quotations in critical publications or reviews, no part of this book may be reproduced in any manner without prior written permission from the publisher. Write: Permissions, Wipf and Stock Publishers, 199 W. 8th Ave., Suite 3, Eugene, OR 97401.

Wipf & Stock
An Imprint of Wipf and Stock Publishers
199 W. 8th Ave., Suite 3
Eugene, OR 97401

www.wipfandstock.com

PAPERBACK ISBN: 978-1-6667-1520-0
HARDCOVER ISBN: 978-1-6667-1521-7
EBOOK ISBN: 978-1-6667-1522-4

02/09/22

To Elisabeth Sophia Lee, Grace Ji-Sun Kim, Grace Lung,
Haejeong Sue Park, Hanna Hyun, Jessie Giyou Kim, Naomi
Faith Bu, and Sarang Kim,
whose lives and grace inspire me to follow Jesus Christ
—Graham Joseph Hill

To Yeunsuck Lee and Jaemoon Kim,
who teach me the love of Jesus Christ
—Jessie Giyou Kim

Contents

Series Preface	xiii
Foreword by Grace Lung	xxi
Foreword by Hanna Hyun	xxv
1. Sunburnt Country: Changes in Australian Society and Church	1
2. Sweeping Pains: Experiences of Asian Australian Women	18
3. Far Horizons: Women are the Heartbeat of Living Faith	67
Afterword by Grace Ji-Sun Kim	99
Appendix 1: 21 Asian Australian Women Leaders and Theologians You Should Know	101
Appendix 2: 18 Asian and Asian Diaspora Women Theologians You Should Know	117
Appendix 3: Women Theologians of Global Christianity	119
Appendix 4: Questions Used in the Surveys and In-Depth Interviews	124
Authors and Contributors	128
More Books by Graham Joseph Hill	131
Bibliography	133

Series Preface

SERIES: "FAITH AND JUSTICE IN THESE LANDS NOW CALLED AUSTRALIA"

This series explores issues of faith and justice in these lands now called Australia. Each book in the series examines a particular topic of injustice in these lands now called Australia and asks how Christian faith and discipleship shape a just response. But we cannot understand any wrong in this country without facing and acknowledging racist practices and attitudes of governments, churches, and institutions—racism firstly and overwhelmingly directed toward Aboriginal and Torres Strait Islander peoples. Racism in this country has flourished because of the problematic relationship between the church, society, and government. Racism toward Aboriginal and Torres Strait Islander peoples in this country is often unacknowledged, denied, justified, or explained away—and Christians and their leaders are too often involved in this behavior. But racism in this country is endemic. Sometimes, it manifests itself in church cultures, theological systems, educational curricula, and government legislation and policies. This racism is always present in colonizing imaginations.

Series Preface

Each book in this series is peer reviewed under the oversight of an editorial board. The peer-review process ensures quality research and writing, aids in vetting and selecting books for publication, and provides suggestions for improving the books accepted in the series. This process enhances the quality of the books published in this series.

This series considers a wide range of injustices, inequalities, and oppressions in these lands now called Australia. The editors invite and welcome contributions from authors from many Christian traditions, ethnicities, and theological backgrounds. These authors will reflect on contemporary issues through the lens of Christian faith and biblical justice. Authors may explore such topics as Aboriginal and Torres Strait Islander experiences and contributions, homelessness, women's rights and women in leadership, family and domestic violence, mission and discipleship, bullying and harassment, multiculturalism and ethnic diversity, sex and gender issues, refugees and asylum seekers, disability rights, climate change and environmental protection, security and terrorism, unemployment and job security, political polarization, church decline and health, faith in a secular age, leadership scandals and church abuse, and more. Some authors will come specifically from the perspective of decolonization, whereas others will draw from different theological methods and epistemologies. However, all authors in the series will seek to engage critically with culture, Bible, and theology, and acknowledge that all faith and justice exercised in this country occurs on Aboriginal and Torres Strait Islander lands.

This series applies diverse frames of reference to multiethnic, secular, and pluralistic modernity as it reveals itself in these lands now called Australia. Therefore, an Indigenous and decolonizing viewpoint is one lens among many in this series. But as Dr. Garry Deverell (a member of the series editorial board) reminds us: "The colonial imaginary may still be at work in such perspectives and the series needs to be mindful of that fact."

We cannot consider injustices in this country without first seeing the primary and original sin directed towards the Aboriginal and Torres Strait Islander peoples. "Australia" is a colonial project where racism and injustice are alive and well. The racial inequities

Series Preface

of this colonial nation established themselves when the country was invaded on the lie of terra nullius and express themselves as stolen land, stolen wages, stolen lives, stolen generations, Aboriginal deaths in custody, overrepresentation in prison systems, the destruction of sacred sites, and shameful treatment of Aboriginal and Torres Strait Islander women, children, men, and families. This structural injustice is pervasive, colonial, sinful, and disgraceful, and Christians often perpetuate the problem. To protest the mistreatment of Aboriginal and Torres Strait Islander peoples is to partake in righteous anger—anger shared by God. There is no reconciliation without repentance and reparations and the recognition of Aboriginal and Torres Strait Islander peoples in the Constitution.

Dr. Garry Deverell, Indigenous theologian and author of *Gondwana Theology* (2018) and *The Bonds of Freedom* (2008), also reminds us that "Australia" is a colonial project rooted in the injustices, lies, and racism we have mentioned. Instead of "Australia," Dr. Deverell wonders if terms like "Gondwana" might evoke a more ancient, Indigenous sensibility concerning the continent on which we all now live (Gondwana being a reference to the ancient supercontinent that broke up about 180 million years ago and included the lands of this continent). "Gondwana" is rarely used in this way. Still, it distinguishes these lands and their peoples from the colonial project called "Australia," which perpetuates ongoing injustices against Aboriginal and Torres Strait Islander peoples.

Dr. Deverell expresses that "the only way to appreciate the injustices and possibilities of this nation is through close attention to the long history of this continent's Aboriginal and Torres Strait Islander peoples. The first issue to be confronted by any proposed series on "Australian" theology is the problematic nature of "Australia" as a colonial project. If this is not done, then every other issue addressed will repeat the ontological and epistemological practices of dispossession and displacement, which are the true font and source of every other "Australian" theology. Once Australians have acknowledged and rejected the colonial project and all that came with it, then we can genuinely respond to other injustices in our nation in the light of Christian faith—asylum seekers and refugees, domestic and family violence, racism toward people of colour, modern slavery, religious and ethnic discrimination, ageism and ableism, inequalities and biases experienced by women of colour, sexual and gender oppression, climate and environmental degradation, poverty and economic injustice, homelessness, child abuse and neglect, and more.

This series seeks to critically engage Australian colonialism and its imagination, beliefs, practices, and racism. Sometimes we will get that right. At other times we will fail and need to repent of our colonial imaginations and ask for forgiveness. Not every book in this series will explicitly consider Aboriginal and Torres Strait Islander matters. But every issue will, through the lens of the Christian faith, address issues of injustice among groups in these lands now called Australia.

The authors in this series won't just focus on injustice. They will also examine a biblical theology of justice and highlight ways God's people are already working toward justice, peacemaking, healing, and reconciliation in these lands now called Australia.

The Bible affirms that God cares deeply about justice and calls his people to act justly and work toward a just society. The Lord has shown us, "what is good. And what does the Lord require of you? To act justly and to love mercy and to walk humbly with your God" (Mic 6:8). He calls us to "Learn to do right; seek justice. Defend the oppressed. Take up the cause of the fatherless; plead the case of the widow" (Isa 1:17). He has commanded us to "Administer true justice; show mercy and compassion to one another. Do not oppress the widow or the fatherless, the foreigner or the poor. Do not plot evil against each other" (Zech 7:9–10). The Lord has given us no other option but to "Speak up for those who cannot speak for themselves, for the rights of all who are destitute. Speak up and judge fairly; defend the rights of the poor and needy" (Prov 31:8–9). The Lord, our God, commands us to "Defend the weak and the fatherless; uphold the cause of the poor and oppressed" (Ps 82:3).

Churches that follow these commands are prophetic and self-giving, radical and activistic, and wild and dangerous. They are churches filled with transformed nonconformists (Rom 12:2).

The Bible repeatedly urges us to embrace God's heart for justice and mercy. There are more than two thousand verses in the

Series Preface

Bible on poverty and justice. Our world is crying out for justice. Jesus calls us to be a prophetic church committed to justice and compassion.

Recently I had a conversation with Scot McKnight, who is a leading New Testament scholar and author. He commented on how often the Law and Prophets combine God's will (*mishpat*, etc.) with righteousness and justice (*tsedeq, tsedaqah*) and how wide-ranging that *tsedeq* is. Deuteronomy 16:19-20 says, "Do not pervert justice or show partiality . . . Follow justice and justice alone, so that you may live and possess the land the Lord your God is giving you." Amos 5:24 uses *mishpat* and *tsedeq* in parallel and could be read as "Let 'judgment' and 'justice' roll down like waters, and 'right conduct' and 'righteousness' like an ever-flowing stream." Doing justice involves both good judgment and right conduct in acting with and on behalf of the disadvantaged in societies. Furthermore, the righteous will and judgment of God is the source of our concern for justice. Time and again, the Law and the Prophets say that God's will is that his people be a people of righteous conduct and judgment and compassionate justice.

Governments, businesses, and humanitarian organizations have an essential role to play in addressing poverty and injustice. But the church must never lose sight of its function. There is no redemption by government; there is only redemption in Christ. In many Christian circles, mission and evangelism are out, while social justice is popular. But true justice always combines social concern and activism with gospel proclamation, biblical faithfulness, evangelism and mission, and healthy church life. The local church is paramount in God's mission. Humans need justice and liberation, but they also need personal redemption. This is not a matter of *either-or*. We are *first* the church of Jesus Christ, witnessing to Jesus's redemption, gospel, and justice through our life together and in the world. We are *then* the church that serves among and influences governments and other organizations. This is not a matter of *either*-or but one of *first-then*.

God calls Christians to respond to poverty and injustice (Prov 14:31; 19:17; 21:13; 28:27; Isa 58:6-10; Hos 6:6; Amos 5:24; Mic 6:8). "He has told you, O mortal, what is good. And what does the

Series Preface

Lord require of you? But to do justice, to love kindness, and to walk humbly with your God?" (Mic 6:8). The Scriptures are full of such appeals. These appeals to do justice and love mercy span the Law, the historical books, the poetic books and wisdom literature, the Prophets, the life and teaching of Jesus Christ, the example of the New Testament Church, and the Pauline Epistles and the book of James. God is a just and compassionate God who calls his people to be just, kind, and humble.

In Luke 4:18–19, Jesus echoes the words of Isaiah 61, including the proclamation of good news for the poor and the Lord's love for justice. The Lord "upholds the cause of the oppressed, gives food to the hungry, sets prisoners free, gives sight to the blind, lifts up those who are bowed down, watches over the foreigner, sustains the fatherless and the widow, and loves the righteous" (Ps 146:5–9). The Messiah, who is God's chosen Servant, "proclaims justice to the nations," caring for the bruised and broken (Matt 12:15–21). Jesus condemns religious leaders and institutions that neglect justice, mercy, and faithfulness (Matt 23:23). Jesus makes it clear: ". . . whatever you did for one of the least of these brothers and sisters of mine, you did it for me" (Matt 25:40).

Jesus challenges his people to respond to injustice and show God's peace, justice, and reconciliation—this is at the heart of discipleship and the gospel. The prophetic church sees this and responds. God calls us to proclaim and usher in a new age of justice, equality, healing, and freedom.

The books in this series don't merely focus on injustices in these lands now called Australia and necessary responses by those of the Christian faith. Authors also explore how God's people are already seeking to be voices for justice in this nation—speaking up for the poor, protesting the treatment of asylum seekers and refugees, feeding the hungry, housing the homeless, protecting vulnerable women and children, loving neighbors, welcoming and advocating for religious and ethnic minorities, providing affordable food and healthcare, engaging in political and policy advocacy, building communities, and more.

The vision of the series is for *faith and justice in these lands now called Australia*—justice first for the land and the sovereign

Series Preface

people who belong to this country and then for other marginalized and vulnerable groups. Jesus calls his disciples to love mercy, seek justice, and walk humbly with their God. This series explores that call and shows how God's people are responding with courage and conviction.

Rev. Dr. Graham Joseph Hill
Principal and Associate Professor of Global Christianity
Stirling College (University of Divinity)
Editor in Chief

Foreword by Grace Lung

Concerned for the growth of Asian Australian Christianity, I had just finished a stint at Fuller Theological Seminary's Asian American program and embarked on a journey to contextualize learnings from the American to the Australian context. This involved writing for various Christian websites and creating resources for the Asian Australian churches here. All the while, I was looking for others who shared the same desire to look at faith from a minority point of view in Australia.

So, I was delighted to stumble across various interviews by Majority World Christians on Graham Joseph Hill's *The Global Church Project* website. I was even more amazed to discover that there was an Anglo-Australian behind the endeavor! In the videos, Graham's warmth and down-to-earth image hid his immense expertise, global reach, and long list of qualifications. Rather than the typical Western white male expert being the source of knowledge and model, I realized there was a white, male expert here who wanted to listen and learn from what minority voices had to contribute; that he thought *we* had something meaningful to offer to global Christianity and was driven by a mission to amplify these voices.

As Graham compiled his *Women in Theology in Australia and New Zealand* list for the site, we connected directly later, and I was stunned that he intended to include *me* on the list. From then on, Graham has been a key encourager and enabler of my decision to pursue higher degree research and academic writing, despite my doubts and insecurities.

People often comment that in my work, I have given voice or words to their experiences. Hearing them said aloud and published makes them tangible and shareable. This is what Graham Joseph Hill and Jessie Giyou Kim achieve expertly through this book by drawing on reliable data and featuring the voices of Asian Australian women themselves. Good data is hard to access, and the book shows a fuller picture of Asian Australian women than is often depicted. Diversity is essential because, within our sub-tribes, my limited experience can easily inform me: Hong Kong Chinese, second-generation, middle to upper class, and Protestant view. The book enabled me to see the diversity of Asian Australian workers beyond our tribes, working in different contexts, different roles, beyond children's and hospitality stereotypes (as crucial as they are), and features both first- and second-generation perspectives. Within here are voices that remind me that I have marginalized myself.

In addition, the book presents feelings I have felt and are familiar to many women—of true joy in service and support and encouragement received from their churches on missions and ministry work. At the same time, they are openly revealing the lived experiences of inequalities and vulnerabilities as women and minorities. The women interviewed have a safe space to really "spill the tea"! The thoughts shared here are usually confined internally, shared in prayers to the Father, in hushed tones, or tears to just one specially selected confidant. The honesty here is rare, valuable, and insightful. A significant number of us have experienced these realities firsthand, but it can be challenging to articulate. When it can be expressed, others may try to speak for us, whether it is a spouse or majority race leaders. We are taught to accept this and to normalize it.

Consequently, many of us are ill-prepared because we are blind to these vulnerabilities and brokenness until it's too late—it impacts our spiritual lives, our ministries, our mental health. There are real wounds here; racism, sexism, and inequalities have been voiced in this book, and training institutions and faith communities should take note. However, rather than condemnation, there is hope, and

Foreword by Grace Lung

achievable steps as Graham and Jessie provide a practical theology to address these inequalities in an intelligent and empowering way.

It is a shame that many Asian Australian Christian women do not have opportunities to reflect on these realities, not in our training or on the field. Not in women's conferences here in Australia, not even in women's events in our churches, ethnic or not. Furthermore, having been in Asian Australian church ministry for over twenty years, I've not come across any published books on our faith community. This should not be, considering the high number of Asian Australians raised and working in the harvest. Until now.

As a book that features research on Asian Australian women, the title *Sunburnt Country, Sweeping Pains* is striking. Graham and Jessie locate their work within the changing Australian context. Rather than being relegated to a corner for those "others" and by those "others" only, the research has a direct and fitting bearing on the Australian and First Nations context. I pray that many people from all sorts of cultural backgrounds pick up, learn, and embrace the practical steps given in this book. Then go and be agents of change in their ministry contexts while engaging entrenched, unequal systems.

Graham and Jessie's work here is a significant piece of research that I will be drawing on in my own work. I sincerely hope this book will be joined soon by many others to develop this vital discipline of Asian Australian Christianity for generations to come. I can't thank them both enough for championing this voice and beginning to fill in this gaping void in such a considered, expert, and humble way.

So—the first book on Asian Australian Christians! I'm so incredibly thankful and shouldn't have been surprised that God has brought to the forefront those who can be relegated to the background—serving busily, unassumingly, and faithfully—beloved daughters of the Father.

Grace Lung
The Asians Between Cultures Course
Brisbane, Australia

Foreword by Hanna Hyun

It has been two years since I left Australia. In my mind, I can still see Bondi Beach, the vast wineries, and lush giant forests. Above all, getting to know Graham was a blessing. As I read through this publication by Graham Joseph Hill and Jessie Giyou Kim, I considered the hardships Asian women face in Australia through the lens of my personal experiences there. I saw many women reluctantly entering an academic program or seeking employment as a stepping-stone to immigration. Others accepted exploitative labor contracts to support the family they left behind in their home country. Australia seems beautiful, welcoming, and peaceful to visitors. Still, Aboriginal and Torres Strait Islanders, the original inhabitants and caretakers of the land, would almost certainly disagree with this assessment of the society now settled by white people.

Living in Australia for five years as an Asian woman theologian enabled me to witness different aspects of Australian society. Living in Australia has also made me appreciate how Graham and Jessie have gathered the voices of Asian women in Australia. In a society still struggling to accept its ethnic minorities, this book encourages Asian women to stand courageous as leaders, and I hear it as the voice of Christ. As Graham tells us, it isn't only Asian and other immigrant women who exist on the margins of Australian society. Women, Indigenous peoples, and others are marginalized. Many women who were born and raised in Australia remain at the margins of society. Women are given a seat at the table only when they take on heavy responsibilities. But when they seek leadership positions, they are barred from making their voices heard among the white and primarily male establishment. The sad stories of the many women recounted in this book tell us that the multicultural Australian society still must provide equal opportunity for different voices to be heard. The stereotypical image of an Asian woman with a soft voice and submissive demeanor tending to her home and supporting her husband does not apply to so many women of Asian ethnicity.

Inequality also exists in immigrant churches where Asian male leaders often take all the leadership positions in academia and churches and do not rightfully acknowledge Asian women's ministerial or theological contributions. Women are unfairly assessed or not given an equal chance for promotion (these are often ways men protect their vested interests). Having been dominated by white people, Asian men often turn to Asian women to exploit them or use them for their own gains and successes. In Christ, we are free and are one. As Galatians 3:28 says, males and females must enjoy equality in Christ. But because the reality has not been so, the women's voices in this book—a book written by a white man (Graham) and an Asian woman (Jessie)—are even more valuable. Considering Jesus's command to "go and do likewise" (Luke 10), this book by Graham and Jessie is a work of research that expresses Christ's authentic love for the immigrant women and their children. These immigrant women are the twenty-first-century version of the ones robbed in the streets and passed over by the teachers of the law.

In Sydney, I spent most of my time with women from the Middle East, especially Syrian refugees who settled between 2016 and 2019. I have fond memories of my time with the women who left their country to settle in Australia for political or religious reasons. This book contains stories of numerous Asian women and their children who have legal residency status in Australia but have difficulty adapting to society because of language difficulties and culture shock. The many siloed Asian immigrant communities in the numerous Australian suburbs struggle to build themselves up.

FOREWORD BY HANNA HYUN

Moreover, their struggle is often born by the backs, work, and tears of Asian women and children and their countless sacrifices. The book you hold in your hand is one that genuinely sees their hardships and washes away their hidden tears.

Hanna Hyun
Ansan, South Korea

1

Sunburnt Country

Changes in Australian Society and Church

A RAPIDLY CHANGING, MULTIETHNIC, AND MULTICULTURAL AUSTRALIA

Australia is a culturally diverse nation and home to the oldest known continuing culture on Earth. "A new genomic study has revealed that Aboriginal Australians are the oldest known civilization on Earth, with ancestries stretching back roughly 75,000 years . . . The data may show Aboriginal Australians came to the continent as early as 31,000 years ago."[1]

While being home to this ancient and beautiful culture, data also shows rapid and substantial changes in churches and society in the lands we now call Australia. The Australian Bureau of Statistics reports, "In 2020, there were over 7.6 million migrants living in Australia. This was 29.8 percent of the population that were born overseas. One year earlier, in 2019, there were 7.5 million people born overseas. Nearly every single country from around the world

---

1. Jozuka, "Aboriginal Australians."

was represented in Australia's population in 2020."[2] While people from the United Kingdom continue to be the largest group migrating to Australia, the second largest group is Indian and the third largest, Chinese. Migration from China, India, the Philippines, Vietnam, Malaysia, and Sri Lanka occupy six of the ten largest groups migrating to Australia in 2020.

When one looks at the top twenty countries of birth in Australia, half of these countries are in Asia.[3] In 2020, 8.9 percent of Australia's population were born in Asia. Furthermore, 47 percent of Australians born overseas say they are Christian. We live in the Australian state of New South Wales (NSW). The largest group of overseas-born residents in NSW are Chinese: 256,000 people in 2020. Jessie lives in Macquarie Park NSW, where 68.2 percent of people were born overseas, including over 33 percent in China, India, South Korea, the Philippines, and Hong Kong. Graham lives in North Epping NSW, where almost 20 percent of people were born in China, India, Hong Kong, or South Korea. In greater Epping NSW, 58.6 percent of people were born overseas, mainly in Asia. The World Christian Encyclopedia says that in 2020, 77.4 percent of people living in Oceania report to be Christian.[4] In Asia, "Christians grew twice as fast as the general population over the 20th century and represent 8.2% of Asia's population in 2020 . . . The highest growth rate among Christian families from 1970–2020 (15.4% p.a.) was among the house churches, particularly in China. Though this growth has slowed considerably since 2015, 56 million Christians still worship in house churches in Asia."[5] Ethnically Asian churches are multiplying in Australia and are reshaping the church. As one news article recently announced, the future of the Australian church is Asian.[6]

Australian church life and ethnic diversity are rapidly changing, therefore. But few studies have been conducted looking at the

---

2. Australian Bureau of Statistics, "Migration, Australia."
3. Australian Bureau of Statistics, "Statistics."
4. Johnson and Zurlo, *World Christian Encyclopedia*, 18.
5. Johnson and Zurlo, *World Christian Encyclopedia*, 10–11.
6. Payne, "Future of the Church."

contributions and experiences of Asian Australian Christians in local church ministry and overseas missions.

This book seeks to contribute to this research area by examining the experiences and contributions of Asian Australian women in ministry and mission, including their experiences of inequality, racism, sexism, vulnerability, and stereotypes. The book's title and section headings adapt the much-loved second stanza of Australian Dorothea Mackellar's poem *My Country*.[7] Examining National Church Life Survey (NCLS) 2016 data and in-depth surveys and interviews, this volume considers the contributions and experiences of these Asian Australian women. We propose ways of dealing with the sexism, racism, and inequalities these women face. Releasing these women fully to ministry and mission enriches the church and its mission.

EXPRESSING THIRD-CULTURE IDENTITY AND THEOLOGY

Like most migrants and their descendants, Asian Australian women seek to forge their identity, beliefs, and culture in new social and cultural contexts.[8] These women, and especially second and third generations, are often bicultural. They value their Asian ethnic, cultural, and linguistic heritage while closely identifying with a diverse, pluralistic, multiethnic, multicultural Australian nation, church, and society. The *Australian Survey of Social Attitudes* (AuSSA) is a biennial survey studying Australians' social attitudes and behaviors. Examining the findings of AuSSA of 273 Asian Australians, university researchers concluded:

> In terms of multiculturalism, the expression of cultural diversity among Asian Australian migrants (i.e., maintaining one's birth language and cultural heritage) does not tend to have a causal effect on whether Asian Australian migrants are more or less likely to feel a sense of connection or belonging to Australian identity. Therefore,

---

7. Mackellar, *My Country*, st. 2.
8. Kwai, "Young Asian-Australians." See Winarnita, "Politics and Poetics."

popular representations of multiculturalism as contributing to a fragmented and fractured national identity do not always hold up with statistical analysis.[9]

Young Asian Australians shape unique bicultural, third-culture identities. Still, they often do this while valuing their Asian ancestry and heritage and embracing their sense of belonging to a diverse, pluralistic, globalized, multicultural, and multireligious Australia.

Many second- and third-generation Asian Australians are third-culture individuals (TCI) with unique third-culture identities. Raised in a culture other than the culture of their parents or ancestors and living between that world and Australian society, they are often bilingual or multilingual, bicultural, open to plurality and diversity, and given to creativity, originality, and inclusivity. Given this is the case, Asian Australians can model, and help Christians live out, a bicultural, hospitable, innovative, and third-culture Christian faith. Ruth Padilla DeBorst challenges churches to develop disciples and fellowships that are third culture. By this, she means that Christians must embrace the culture of the Christian faith. But they must also engage "meaningfully, and with a sense of belonging, with people from very diverse cultural backgrounds."[10] (As an example DeBorst uses third-culture children, i.e., those who grow up with two cultures. They find meaningful and creative ways to put these cultures into dialogue.) God calls the church to be a diverse, inclusive, migrant, third-culture people. DeBorst puts it this way:

> God's kingdom is not some amorphous, supra-cultural, other-world milieu. Rather, it is a space of vibrant, life-giving, God honoring encounter of spice and colour, smell and sound, here and now, in the complex entanglement of human relations. As third-culture people, followers of Jesus are called to live today in the light of the completion of God's story, with daily expectation of Christ's imminent return. They are called to express in their daily interactions, the confident belief that one day the triumphal choir before God's throne will be composed of a great multitude from every nation, tribe, and people,

---

9. Clark, "Perceptions," 315. See ACSPRI, "Australian Survey."
10. DeBorst, "'Unexpected' Guests," 73.

proclaiming, on bended knee, God's sovereignty in their own distinct languages . . . In as far as Christian communities the world over live together in light of God's gracefull story, they become historically visible and culturally alternative out-workings of God's mission and localized expressions of the bountiful banquet of God's kingdom.[11]

Tseen-Ling Khoo uses the phrase "banana bending" to signify how Asian Australians and Asian Canadians merge Asian and Western cultures and identities while "bending" political and social expectations and systems of discrimination, stereotyping, sexism, racism, politicization, and oppression. Peeling back the layers of nation, community, and gender, Khoo challenges the politics of racialization and invites us into a critical appreciation for diasporic Asian culture and literature.[12]

There are great lessons here for the Australian church. Instead of embracing the politics of racialization or the values and outlook of the dominant culture, Asian Australian women challenge us to: (1) embrace diversity and plurality; (2) reject racialized, nationalistic, sexualized, and politicized narratives; (3) nurture bicultural, migrant, diaspora, hybrid, third-culture identities; (4) recognize unity in difference; (5) see ethics and hospitality as inseparable since hospitality is central to Christian ethics; (6) pursue a Pentecostal disposition, which celebrates unity in diversity; (7) appreciate that migrant and host are both equal recipients and givers of hospitality and grace; and (8) find new life, fresh theology, Pentecostal community, and transformed identity in the marginalized voices and liminal experiences. As Lesley Houston says, "God's people need to live with marginality and liminality as a permanent, safe, transforming, third space. Being third culture people means seeing liminality as a set way of life, embracing the holy insecurity of liminal existence, and embarking on the quest for freedom to live in a world of ambiguity. Essentially, this is about naming the third space and third culture as safe, renewing, and God's space and culture."[13]

---

11. DeBorst, "'Unexpected' Guests," 75–76.
12. Khoo, *Banana Bending*.
13. Houston, "Marginality, Liminality."

CHALLENGING STEREOTYPES, RACIALIZATION, AND SEXUALIZATION

Asian Australian women can be caught between the restrictive, historical Asian conceptions of gender and prevailing, damaging Western stereotypes. Both forms of gender stereotyping, sexualization, and discrimination can be painful for women.

We begin with Asian historical, religious, and cultural notions of gender and sexuality. This, of course, is a vast field, spanning thousands of years, many religions, and numerous Asian cultures. The picture is a complex one. In many Asian societies and historical eras, women experienced gender oppression, relational disadvantage, political exploitation, religious discrimination, and sexual objectification. Women were often defined by kinship and domestic roles: mother, sister, daughter, wife, daughter-in-law, mother-in-law, maid, and so on. Yet Asian women also contributed to their societies, people groups, and religions in striking ways—as poets, politicians, philosophers, authors, and more. Throughout history, most Asian women have been subjected to gender discrimination, and the problem continues. The World Economic Forum *Global Gender Gap Report 2021* notes:

> There are significant disparities across and within various geographies. Western Europe remains the region that has progressed the most towards gender parity (77.6 percent) and is further progressing this year. North America is the second-most advanced (76.4 percent), also improving this year, followed by Latin America and the Caribbean (72.1 percent) and Eastern Europe and Central Asia (71.2 percent). A few decimal points below is the East Asia and the Pacific region (68.9 percent), one of the most-improved regions, just ahead of Sub-Saharan Africa (67.2 percent) and surpassing South Asia (62.7 percent). The Middle East and North Africa region remains the area with the largest gap (60.9 percent).
>
> At the current relative pace, gender gaps can potentially be closed in 52.1 years in Western Europe, 61.5 years in North America, and 68.9 years in Latin America and the Caribbean. In all other regions it will take over

100 years to close the gender gap: 121.7 years in Sub-Saharan Africa, 134.7 years in Eastern Europe and Central Asia, 165.1 years in East Asia and the Pacific, 142.4 years in Middle East and North Africa, and 195.4 years in South Asia.[14]

In 2017, Lily Xiao Hong Lee and Sue Wiles edited a collection of thirteen papers for the *Journal of the Oriental Society of Australia* under a special issue called "Gender in Asian Society and Culture." Both are scholars with expertise on China who are researching the experiences of Chinese women and are concerned to analyze and redress gender inequalities in Asia and Australia. The thirteen papers cover vast historical and cultural territory and show how Asian women have faced and sought to overcome gender discrimination throughout history. Here are a few examples of the articles in this extraordinary collection: (1) Barbara Hendrischke's outline of Han Fei's philosophical engagement with women's lives and intellectual contributions, including consorts, daughters, mothers, and wives (third century BCE); (2) Qiaomei Tang's examination of Chinese gender relationships, cultural elitism, and political power through the lens of a sixth-century CE divorce case; (3) Lily Xiao Hong Lee's consideration of Chinese courtesans' role as performers and possibly authors of lyrics to songs during the late Tang era in China (seventh century CE); (4) Tin Kei Wong's analysis of the representations of the female emperor Wu Zetian (who reigned in China from 690 to 705 CE) as an insatiable erotic woman and a strong sovereign leader—both images are revealing patriarchal ideologies and common approaches to delegitimizing female leadership; (5) Yanning Wang's focus on the maids of wealthy, educated, cloistered Chinese women and their experiences of influence, exploitation, and mutual dependence on these literati women; and (6) Ng Mei-Kwan's study of Yuan Mei's protégées and Chinese female poetry societies. "Through seeking discipleship, studying poems, forming poetry societies, and putting to good use their kinship and geographic networks, these female literati morphed from talented women confined to the inner chambers into a creative community in literary circles. Their works

---

14. World Economic Forum, *Global Gender Gap Report 2021*, 7.

thereby became cultural assets for all, which in turn legitimized their literary pursuits with the right to speak for themselves."[15]

Kaku Sechiyama, of the University of Tokyo, offers a comparative sociology of gender and an extensive overview and critical analysis of patriarchy in his book *Higashi Ajia no kafu chōsei: jendā no hikakushakaigaku (East Asian Patriarchal Systems: Comparative Sociology of Gender)*.[16] Unpacking how the notion of patriarchy is understood in the West, Sechiyama then offers an Asian analysis and conceptualization of patriarchy. He then shows how patriarchal ideologies, systems, and institutions express themselves in Confucianism, gender-based allocation of power and roles, views on family and generations, and participation in politics, family, economics, and religion. Sechiyama scrutinizes the forms of patriarchy in Japan, South Korea, Taiwan, North Korea, and China. He then shows how gender discrimination and patriarchal power continue in Asia in women's labor and salaries, domestic and marital expectations, access to education and independence, and who bears the cost of reproduction and social support systems and care. Sechiyama challenges Asian governments and societies to address and move beyond patriarchy.

We need to appreciate how many Asian Australian women struggle with gender discrimination and gender disparity from their cultural backgrounds, even while they experience stereotypes, racialization, and sexualization in Australia. Matthew D. Kim and Daniel L. Wong outline many of the pressures facing diaspora people with an Asian ethnic background, including questions of identity, parental expectations (language, education, career, marriage, children, and parents), church affiliation, the role of women, being a visible and notionally "model" minority, feeling like a perpetual minority, and violence against Asian immigrants, students, and women.[17] Additionally, Asian Australian women face sexual objectification and gender-racial stereotypes.

Shirley Tucker shows how "representations of Asian women in Australian literature have much in common with popular

---

15. Lee and Wiles, "Gender in Asian Society," 29.
16. Sechiyama, *Patriarchy in East Asia*.
17. Kim et al., *Finding Our Voice*, 21–46.

representations of the landscape: both tend to be depicted as highly sexualized, yet passive; erratic, cruel, and unforgiving."[18] Tucker does this by examining the work of four Asian Australian writers: Mena Abdullah, Dewi Anggraeni, Yasmine Gooneratne, and Simone Lazaroo. Through their writings, these Asian Australian women reveal the similarities between Australian notions of landscape and Australian perceptions of Asian girls and women. These women also challenge the white, gendered, Eurocentric vision of country, belonging, identity, and sexuality.

> Because their landscape imagery both exposes and ridicules the specifically gendered and Eurocentric assumptions that have underpinned definitions and representations of "Australianness" and nationhood, much of their work challenges conceptions of Australian identity itself. In this important way, Asian Australian women writers participate in both the myth-making and myth-questioning processes ... [These Asian Australian women use iconic landscape images] to change the prescriptive and limited meanings that have, for too long, characterized and defined Australian literature.[19]

Many Asian Australian women confront oppressive stereotypes. They challenge white, male, Eurocentric, elitist cultural and literary readings of art, society, gender, nation, literature, and "Australianness." Asian Australian women often name the principalities and powers, systems and structures, and ideologies and theologies that support and perpetuate stereotypes, discrimination, racism, and sexism.

RESPONSIBILITY FOR IMPLICIT BIAS, RACISM, AND SEXISM

Asian Australian women often face implicit bias and discrimination in ministry and mission both in Australia and overseas. Bias, racism, prejudice, and sexism are often implicit rather than explicit. Overt

---

18. Tucker, "Great Southern Land," 178.
19. Tucker, "Great Southern Land," 187.

expressions of these things still occur, but it's the implicit stereotyping, systems, and attitudes that do much of the damage to people and our Christian witness. Leaders, participants, and institutions may be unaware of the implicit bias that plagues their organizations, conversations, interactions, relationships, promotions, and decisions. Yet, such implicit prejudice and discrimination is harmful. Implicit Association Tests (IATs) are used to measure implicit bias. Significant peer-reviewed research has been done using IATs over the past twenty years, and IATs continue to improve through rigorous research and experimentation. As data from millions of visitors to the Project Implicit website shows, implicit bias can exist and influence attitudes, behaviors, and decisions, even when people are unaware of such bias in their outlook.[20] Implicit bias based on sexuality, gender, race, ableism, age, or anything else, is unjust, wrong, and harmful. Because the injustices of implicit biases are cumulative, systemic, and collectively perpetuated, they are especially offensive and painful for those subjected to them.

The University of Sheffield researchers Jules Holroyd, Robin Scaife, and Tom Stafford offer an insightful examination of responsibility for implicit bias. They conclude:

> As Madva (2016b) has persuasively argued, attention to individual or collective endeavors should not be seen as competing; rather, the complex interplay between individual and more collective or structural interventions needs to be recognised . . . The overall point, then, is that in recognising the role that individuals and institutions must play, we see that institutional responsibility must reach further than simply providing implicit bias training, on the assumption that this devolves responsibility to individuals for dealing with discrimination. Rather, the responsibility is with (individuals within) institutions to take sustained measures to address whatever mechanisms are producing discriminatory outcomes. Implicit bias training may be a part of those measures, but institutional change must extend well beyond this.[21]

20. Project Implicit, "Project Implicit."
21. Holroyd et al., "Responsibility for Implicit Bias," 10. See Madva,

The responsibility for implicit bias belongs with institutions and with individuals within institutions. Proactive, deliberate, sustained measures need to be taken to deal with implicit bias, racism, discrimination, and sexism in churches and Christian organizations.

DEVELOPING A THEOLOGY OF RACE AND MIGRATION

Dealing with the challenges faced by Asian Australian women and other minoritized groups requires a theology of race and migration. Let's start with a theology of race. Willie James Jennings and J. Kameron Carter make a compelling case for how a theology of race can root Christian identity in the story of the Jewish Jesus, Pentecost, the Eschaton, and the new humanity in Jesus Christ. Willie James Jennings's book *The Christian Imagination: Theology and the Origins of Race* is a theological tour de force. Jennings's theology engages with postcolonial theory, social sciences, history, systematic theology, sociopolitics, and more. Jennings challenges diseased and racialized Christian social imaginations. Jennings says:

> I want Christians to recognize the grotesque nature of a social performance of Christianity that imagines Christian identity floating above land, landscape, animals, place, and space, leaving such realities to the machinations of capitalistic calculations and the commodity chains of private property. Such Christian identity can only inevitably lodge itself in the materiality of racial existence . . . And if, as I believe, Christian life is indeed a way forward for the world, then it must reemerge as a compelling new invitation to life together.[22]

As Grace Ji-Sun Kim and Graham say in *Healing Our Broken Humanity*, we gentiles (North Americans, Australians, New Zealanders, British, Asians, Latin Americans, Africans, etc.) join the story of Jesus. Now, in Jesus Christ, all our personal and corporate

---

"Anti-Anti-Individualism."

22. Jennings, *Christian Imagination*, 293–94.

(including ethnic) stories are situated and framed within the story of biblical Israel, the Jewish Jesus, the new humanity, the new creation, and the age to come. We come together as new humanity and new creation in Jesus, witnessing to Christ's final rule and reign. We express this in grace, love, forgiveness, lament, fellowship, hospitality, welcome, and a commitment to human flourishing.[23]

There is diversity in the church, but it still must become less monocultural and become more intercultural. If the church is indeed the church, then we must be a community of diverse races, languages, cultures, marital statuses, political views, genders, professions, experiences, ages, socioeconomic backgrounds, and much more. Scot McKnight says we are a "fellowship of differents."[24] This means we understand Christian life as fellowship, social revolution, life together, and transcending and honoring and enjoying difference. We know Christian life "to be about love, justice, and reconciliation."[25] This revelation motivates us to be less monoethnic and become an intercultural church. As Christians, we must root our theology of race and commitment to diversity in a profound biblical and theological imagination. "Diversity without theological substance is shallow and secularized. We need a vision of unity in diversity under Christ that is rooted in Scripture and theology."[26]

In *Race: A Theological Account*, J. Kameron Carter challenges racialized Christian imaginations that oppress people and distort the gospel. Carter puts it this way:

> My fundamental contention is that modernity's racial imagination has its genesis in the theological problem of Christianity's quest to sever itself from its Jewish roots. This severance was carried out in two distinct but integrated steps. First, Jews were cast as a race group in contrast to Western Christians, who with the important assistance of the discourses of Christian theology and philosophy, were also subtly and simultaneously cast as a race group in contrast to Western Christians . . . In this

23. Hill and Kim, *Healing Our Broken Humanity*, 23–24.
24. McKnight, *Fellowship of Differents*.
25. McKnight, *Fellowship of Differents*, 21.
26. Hill and Kim, *Healing Our Broken Humanity*, 24.

way, Western culture began to articulate itself as Christian culture (and vice versa), but now—and this is the new moment—through the medium of a racial imagination. Second, having racialized Jews as a people of the Orient and thus Judaism as a "religion" of the East, Jews were then deemed inferior to Christians of the Occident or the West. Hence, the racial imagination (the first step) proved as well to be a racist imagination of white supremacy (the second step). Within the gulf enacted between Christianity and the Jews, the racial, which proves to be a racist, imagination was forged.[27]

A theology of race is inadequate without a theology of migration, as it is through migration, questions of identity, place, belonging, race, prejudice, exclusion, welcome, and hospitality often emerge. Two theologians help us build a theology of migration: Gemma Tulud Cruz (Asian Australian) and Peter C. Phan (Asian American). In *Toward a Theology of Migration*, Cruz shows how migration and social justice are interconnected, as vulnerable peoples are displaced and exploited, migrant women adapt to new threats and opportunities, and Christians advocate for migration justice and reform. Cruz examines how our theology of church and mission must be shaped around themes of migration, as we seek to be a pilgrim people who grow through movement and liminality, as we strive to nurture intercultural churches, and as we foster a Christian spirituality of welcome, diversity, pilgrimage, the new humanity, and unity.[28] Phan says that in an age of migration, we need a "theology of migration" and a "migration theology." Without migration, there would be no world Christianity. "*Migrantness* is therefore a mark of the church and of Christianity itself. The construction of a theology of migration, then, requires a method composed of three mediations: analytic, hermeneutic, and practical. Using this method, the author sketches a theology of God, Christ, Holy Spirit, eschatology, and Christian existence from the perspective of migration."[29] Our God is a migrant (*Deus Migrator*)

---

27. Carter, *Race*, 4.
28. Cruz, *Theology of Migration*; *Intercultural Theology of Migration*.
29. Phan, "Deus Migrator," 845.

who shapes his church and world through migration. This reality requires *the migration of theology and a theology of migration.*[30]

In Australia, any theology of race and migration is impossible without close, respectful attention to Aboriginal and Torres Strait Islander voices, theologies, and experiences. Every Australian Christian should read *The Great White Flood: Racism in Australia* by Anne Pattel-Gray.

> The problem confronting contemporary Australians is their denial of the status and privilege they have inherited from their forebears, and their failure to identify that the Sins of their forebears have now passed on to their children. The most popular statements made over and over again by white Australians are, "I cannot be held responsible for what my forefathers did to the Aboriginal People"; or "We white Australians cannot be made to feel guilty for what our forefathers have done to the Aboriginal People." Australia's failure to repent and convert is the continuation of their sinning.[31]

RESEARCH AIMS, DATA, AND METHODS

Our research for this book sought to answer the research question, "What are the experiences and contributions of Asian Australian women in ministry and mission, including their experiences of inequality, racism, sexism, vulnerability, and stereotypes?" We also explore how the church's witness is enhanced through these Asian Australian women's ministries and how Australian Christianity might deal with the sexism, racism, and inequalities these women face. This research is crucial since so many Asian Australian women serve in mission and ministry in Australia and overseas. Still, their experiences and contributions have never been seriously or comprehensively detailed or reported.

We conducted this research through surveys and interviews. These research methods allowed us to hear these women's

---

30. Phan, "Deus Migrator." Words in italics are from the article's title.
31. Pattel-Gray, *Great White Flood*, 239–40.

experiences and contributions firsthand and in their voices. The University of Divinity Human Research Ethics Committee (HREC) granted human research ethics approval.[32] We supplied all participants with a Participant Information Statement and Implied Consent Form (that is, each of the thirty-six women who completed the sixty-minute surveys and the fifteen women who completed the ninety-minute interviews). In this consent form, participants permitted us to use their responses in a de-identified way and allowed us to quote any of their responses in a de-identified manner.

1. Australian National Church Life Survey (NCLS) 2016 Data

Following is the data we examined in this study.

Christian Church Attenders (Adults)	Abbreviation	Total Number	% First Generation	% Second Generation
Asian Australian Protestant (Female)[33]	AsA PrtF	7,837	86	14
Asian Australian Catholic (Female)	AsA CthF	14,150	92	8
Australian Protestant and Catholic (Female)	All Fem	113,528	-	-
Australian Protestant (Male and Female)	All Prot	152,430	-	-
Australian Protestant and Catholic (Male and Female)	All NCLS	189,751	-	-

NCLS 2016 surveyed 21,987 Protestant and Catholic Asian Australian adult females.

32. University of Divinity (Australia) Human Research Ethics Committee (HREC) approval was received for this research project in 2020: HREC reference number 371/20. Human research was conducted in accordance with the *National Statement on Ethical Conduct in Human Research*.

33. Powell et al., *Research Profile 2020.02*; *Research Profile 2020.01*. Research commissioned for this book's purposes, drawing on data from the National Church Life Survey 2016. Used by written permission.

Female church attenders from the following denominations/movements are represented in the results in this profile: Anglican, Catholic, Lutheran, Presbyterian, Uniting Church, Australian Christian Churches, C3 Church, International Network of Churches, Christian Revival Crusade, Baptist, Churches of Christ, Christian Reformed, Salvation Army, CityLife Church. Countries of birth options in the survey for attenders (first generation) or one of their parents (second generation) included: China/Hong Kong, Korea, Vietnam, Philippines, India/Sri Lanka, Other Asia.[34]

2. Sixty-Minute Surveys of Women in Mission and Ministry

To enhance the research, we conducted thirty-six surveys with the following women:

- Twenty-three Asian Australian women living in Australia, four of which had been involved in overseas mission (18 first generation and 5 second generation)
- Eight Asian Australian women residing outside Australia, due to mission service (4 first generation and 4 second generation)
- Five Asian American women (to get their perspectives on the key issues).

These thirty-six women listed their ethnicities as Chinese (22), Filipino (5), Indian (3), Indonesian (1), Japanese (2), South Korean (2), and Malaysian (1). Only two of these women identified multiple ethnic identities, and they wrote Chinese Australian.

3. Ninety-Minute In-Depth Interviews of Asian Australian Women in Mission and Ministry

We conducted fifteen interviews with ten first-generation and five second-generation women. These fifteen women listed their

---

34. Powell et al., *Research Profile 2020.02*, 2.

ethnicities as Chinese (4), Filipino (3), Indian (2), Indonesian (1), Japanese (2), South Korean (2), and Malaysian (1). None of the women identified multiple ethnic identities. Six of these women were involved in overseas missions, five in local church ministry in Australia, and four in local church ministry and overseas mission equally.

The NCLS 2016 data gave us a broad overview of the contributions and experiences of Asian Australian women in mission and ministry. The sixty-minute surveys (36) and ninety-minute interviews (15) enabled us to go deeper into the gifts, experiences, inequalities, and futures of Asian Australian Christian women in mission and ministry. These surveys and interviews added rich qualitative data to the quantitative data of the NCLS 2016 research.

We've structured this book in a way that allows us to deal with the experiences and contributions of Asian Australian women in mission and ministry and with ways our churches and Christian organizations can respond. Section headings are adapted from lines in Dorothea Mackellar's beloved Australian poem, *My Country*. Section 1 (*Sunburnt Country*) considers the changes in the Australian church and society. Section 2 (*Sweeping Pains*) records the experiences of Asian Australian women in mission and ministry. Section 3 (*Far Horizons*) outlines the contributions of these women and contemplates the future of the Australian church and its ministries, leadership, and witness. We hope this book will amplify the voices and ministries of Asian Australian women and lead to more just, equal, and diverse expressions of Australian church leadership, mission, education, and ministry.

2

Sweeping Pains

Experiences of Asian Australian Women

LISTENING TO THE VOICES OF WOMEN

The stories of Asian Australian women reveal experiences of pain and discrimination but also contribution and hope. Australian Christian churches and leaders must listen and learn from the voices of these women.

This chapter summarizes the NCLS 2016 results and the surveys and interviews we conducted in 2020. We focus on the most relevant results to understand the experiences of Asian Australian women in ministry and mission, the roles they choose or are given in these areas, and their experiences of inequality, racism, sexism, vulnerability, and stereotypes. The results also reveal the solutions to these problems as proposed by Asian Australian women themselves. We then discuss the theological and practical implications of these stories and experiences.

NATIONAL CHURCH LIFE SURVEY (NCLS) IN 2016

Given the NCLS 2016 covers 7,837 Protestant and 14,150 Catholic Asian Australian female adults, this survey affords us unique insights into the contributions, views, and experiences of Asian Australian Christian women. We can also compare these with the data received from the 189,751 surveys completed in total and from the comparative groups.

Leadership and Ministry Roles (Use of Gifts and Skills)

Forty-one percent of *AsA PrtF* said they performed a leadership or ministry role in their church, with the majority leading or assisting in worship services (23 percent), leading children's or youth ministries (15 percent), or leading a small group (11 percent). *AsA CthF* said that their primary leadership or ministry roles were leading or assisting in worship services (16 percent), leading children's or youth ministries (5 percent), or pastoral care and visitation (4 percent).

AsA PrtF involvement in leadership and ministry (41 percent) is similar to *All Fem* (42 percent). Fifty-one percent of *AsA PrtF* said their gifts and skills are used well, compared with 48 percent of *All Fem*. Given the ecclesial structures in Catholicism, the numbers are naturally lower among *AsA CthF*, where 24 percent said they performed a leadership or ministry role. Compare those numbers with *All Prot*, where male and female Protestants are included in the figures. Fifty-one percent say they are involved in leadership and ministry roles, and 55 percent say their gifts and skills are used well.

Protestant and Catholic Australian men have more leadership and ministry opportunities than women do, and certainly more than Asian Australian women, and feel their gifts and skills are better used. *AsA PrtF* (41 percent) have similar rates of involvement in leadership and ministry as *All Fem* (42 percent) but feel their gifts and skills are better used (51 percent compared with 48 percent). *AsA PrtF* and *AsA CthF* have limited opportunities to be included on councils, boards, and eldership and diaconate groups, compared with the opportunities afforded to *All Fem* and *All NCLS*, and certainly compared with *All Prot*.

AsA PrtF are more likely to consider their gifts and skills to be in interpersonal and hospitality ministries (35 percent interpersonal and 43 percent hospitality), including table ministries and caring for the poor, than do *All NCLS* (27 percent interpersonal and 32 percent hospitality).

Values

When asked what they value, *AsA PrtF* said sermons and teaching (50 percent), small groups for prayer and Bible study (29 percent), prayer (27 percent), and contemporary music and worship (22 percent). *AsA CthF* value Eucharist/Holy Communion (56 percent), sermons and teaching (34 percent), prayer (31 percent), and openness to social or cultural diversity (25 percent). *AsA PrtF* (19 percent) and *AsA CthF* (18 percent) report similar concern for broader community care and social justice issues as do *All Fem* (18 percent) and *All NCLS* (19 percent).

Interestingly, *AsA PrtF* and *AsA CthF* are more concerned about nurturing social and cultural diversity (17 percent and 25 percent respectively) than are *All Prot* (11 percent) and *All NCLS* (13 percent). *AsA PrtF* have greater concern for reaching those who do not attend church (18 percent) than do *All Fem* (12 percent) and *All NCLS* (13 percent). But *AsA PrtF* commitment to reaching out to the unchurched is at the same level as *All Prot* (both 18 percent).

One striking finding is the value *AsA PrtF* place on sermons, preaching, and Bible teaching (50 percent), and *AsA CthF* place on the Eucharist (56 percent). These values may reflect the theological, ecclesial, and cultural traditions from which these Asian Australian women come. There is little difference between *AsA PrtF* and *AsA CthF* in the value of outreach, welfare, and social justice compared with *All Prot* and *All NCLS* (except that *AsA CthF* have less concern for reaching the unchurched). The big difference is the extent to which Asian Australian Christian women (both Catholic and Protestant) value social and cultural diversity.

Views on Faith, Belonging, and Serving Together

AsA PrtF are more likely to report that they experienced much growth in their faith through their local church in the past year (37 percent; compared with 28 percent *All NCLS*). *AsA PrtF* are also more likely to self-identify as Evangelical or Pentecostal than do *All Fem* or *All NCLS*. Thirty-seven percent *AsA PrtF* call themselves Evangelical, compared with *All Fem* (17 percent), *All Prot* (32 percent), and *All NCLS* (18 percent). Furthermore, 29 percent *AsA PrtF* call themselves Pentecostal, compared with *All Fem* (16 percent), *All Prot* (30 percent), and *All NCLS* (16 percent). That is perhaps not unsurprising when many congregations of Asian ethnicity are Evangelical or Pentecostal.

When asked about God's importance in their life, *AsA PrtF* (66 percent) and *AsA CthF* (62 percent) report that God is the essential reality in their life. This compares with *All Fem* (57 percent), *All Prot* (62 percent), and *All NCLS* (55 percent) saying the same thing.

Fifty-eight percent of *AsA PrtF* say they have a strong and growing sense of belonging to the local church, compared with *All Fem* (52 percent), *All Prot* (56 percent), and *All NCLS* (50 percent). This sense of belonging to the local church is noticeable. Only 50 percent of *AsA CthF* report the same thing.

Another thing that stands out is the involvement of *AsA PrtF* in prayer and Bible study groups (51 percent), fellowship groups (34 percent), and evangelistic and outreach activities (24 percent). *AsA PrtF* are more likely to be involved in these things than are *All Fem* or *All NCLS*. *All NCLS* report 31 percent, 31 percent, and 17 percent for the same three activities. Asian Australian Protestant females are much more involved in Bible study, prayer and fellowship groups, and outreach activities than the rest of the Australian Christian population. Concerningly, *AsA CthF* report low involvement in these three ministries (12 percent, 17 percent, and 7 percent, respectively). This should once again alert us to the influence of church tradition. Another indicator of the effect of church tradition is the lower rates of participation of *AsA PrtF* (23 percent) and *AsA CthF* (15 percent) in community service, social justice, and welfare activities, compared with *All Fem* (26 percent), *All Prot* (31 percent), and *All NCLS* (25 percent). Asian Australian Protestant Christians seem to place more value on biblical studies and evangelism than they do social justice and community service, which no doubt reflects their main Christian denominational and theological traditions. It is interesting, though, that *AsA CthF* seem to place less value on all these activities than other Australian Christians.

Views on Imaginative and Flexible Innovation

AsA PrtF (89 percent) and *AsA CthF* (85 percent) tend to be more open to the development of new initiatives in ministry and mission in the local church, compared with *All NCLS* (80 percent). Even those that are unsure about change only stand at *AsA PrtF* (11 percent) and *AsA CthF* (15 percent), compared with *All Fem* (18 percent) and *All NCLS* (18 percent).

Views on Mission and Outwardly Focused Activities (Service, Faith Sharing, and Inclusion)

The views and involvement of female Asian Australian Christians in outwardly focused missions, ministries, and activities is fascinating. Again, it offers an exciting study on the influence of gender, culture, and theological tradition on Christians' behavior and outlook. Gender and cultural expectations are apparent in the results. The other thing we may be seeing in these results is relative access to financial, social, language, and other resources. First- and second-generation Asian Australians often have less access to these things than do more established and majority culture groups. More work needs to be done to unpack these findings and what they mean.

In summary, when compared with *All Fem*, *All Prot*, and *ALL NCLS*, Asian Australian adult Christian females (both Protestant and Catholic) are *less likely* to be involved in informal ways of helping others, *less likely* to be regularly involved in local church-based service activities, *less likely* to have ongoing involvement in community groups not connected with the local church, and *less likely* to have strong beliefs about the need for Christians to actively care for the environment. However, they are *more likely* to have cared for the sick, *more likely* to invite people to church, *more likely* to share their faith with others, *more likely* to follow up someone who has drifted away from the church, and *more likely* to include and welcome new Christians and new arrivals to church.

Here are a few examples to illustrate the differences. Twenty-three percent of *AsA PrtF* and 15 percent of *AsA CthF* report that they are regularly involved in community service, social justice, or welfare activities, compared with *All Fem* (26 percent), *All Prot* (31 percent), and *All NCLS* (25 percent). Fifty-three percent of *AsA PrtF* and 53 percent of *AsA CthF* report that they helped others in informal ways in the last year (gave money, visited someone in hospital, gave possessions, contacted a parliamentarian about an issue, etc.), compared with *All Fem* (63 percent), *All Prot* (64 percent), and *All NCLS* (59 percent).

On the other hand, 86 percent of *AsA PrtF* say they are willing to invite non-believing friends and relatives to a church service, compared with *All Fem* (74 percent), *All Prot* (81 percent), and *All NCLS* (72 percent). Twenty-four percent of *AsA PrtF* report regular involvement in outreach or evangelistic activities, compared with *All Fem* (18 percent) and *All NCLS* (17 percent). Seventy-six percent of *AsA PrtF* and 75 percent of *AsA CthF* say they are ready and at ease with sharing their Christian faith with others and look for opportunities or make the most of them when they arise, compared with *All Fem* (74 percent), *All Prot* (73 percent), and *All NCLS* (71 percent). Twenty-five percent of *AsA PrtF* and 24 percent of *AsA CthF* actively look for opportunities to share their faith, compared with *All Fem* (19 percent) and *All NCLS* (18 percent).

SURVEYS AND INTERVIEWS IN 2020

We conducted thirty-six surveys over sixty minutes (using Survey Monkey) and fifteen interviews over ninety minutes (using Zoom) to dig deeper into the contributions, experiences, inequalities, and futures of Asian Australian Christian women in mission and ministry. These surveys and interviews added rich qualitative data to the quantitative data of the NCLS research. All those who completed the surveys and interviews self-identify as Asian Australian women in ministry or mission. One of the differences between the NCLS surveys and our in-depth surveys and interviews is that the NCLS surveyed all kinds of women with Asian ethnic backgrounds in Australian Christian churches. In contrast, we only conducted surveys and interviews with women of an Asian ethnic background who had gone into ministry or mission. So, our sample is a select group whose experiences are informative but may not represent all women in Australian churches with an Asian ethnic background. This ability to compare information is one of the benefits of putting the NCLS data and the data from our interviews and surveys side by side. The quotations in the following sections come from the surveys and interviews and are used with consent from the participants.

Parental and Church Support

Most of these women felt that their parents were supportive or very supportive of their choice to serve in local ministry or overseas missions (53 percent). Twenty-five percent said their parents were neutral, and 22 percent opposed. Supportive parents encouraged faith in God and a heart for missions and ministry. Parental concerns included safety, financial security, relinquishing a career, wasting an education, and asking others for money. Only 61 percent of these women had both parents who were Christian, and 17 percent did not have Christian parents. Eighty-six percent said their parents did not determine or guide their decision about where they served and what organization.

One woman wrote, "I was discouraged from going to Bible college. So, in discussions with an Asian mentor, we tried to come up with different studying and university solutions so that my parents would be okay with it. For instance, choosing a Bible college that was affiliated with a good university."[1] Another woman recounted a conversation with her mother, who had a personal revelation that

---

1. Research participant fourteen.

her daughter would serve God in overseas missions. "My mother didn't tell me about her revelation until I was on my way to the mission field."[2]

Most of these women (86 percent) reported that their churches supported or greatly supported them in local ministry or overseas missions. Fourteen percent said their churches were neutral on the matter, and there were no reports of churches who were negative or unsupportive. It seems that these women received more support from their churches than their families when it came to choosing a life in ministry or missions.

Opportunities and Choice in Service

When choosing a ministry or mission location to serve, 64 percent of the women said their existing church community or mission agency did not determine or guide their decision about where they served. The 36 percent of women who felt otherwise is not an insignificant number, but freedom of choice was present in most cases.

We asked the women whether race and gender were factors in choosing their ministry or mission agency. Forty-seven percent said these were factors, 39 percent said these were not factors, and 14 percent were neutral. Asked the same question about the role of race and gender when choosing a location to serve, 31 percent said these were factors, 60 percent said these were not factors, and 9 percent were neutral. Two of the women commented on their Chinese ethnicity and language abilities and how these played a role in them choosing to serve among Chinese ethnic groups. One said she was mentored by an Asian leader who guided her to serve in Asia. Another said that her denomination chooses where people will serve, and "they tend to send people back to their cultural or ethnic backgrounds."[3] Another wrote, "Race was mainly the factor in terms of the people group I chose to serve among, but gender was also a determiner of where and with what ministry I served."[4] One

2. Research participant three.
3. Research participant twenty.
4. Research participant twenty-eight.

woman said she chose Asia because of her love for urban culture. Another spoke of the support of her father. "My father was a pastor who was very supportive of women in ministry. It is not always common for pastoral fathers to be as supportive of daughters going into ministry in Chinese culture."[5]

The pathway into service was not always smooth for these women. "I was asked which region in the world I could see myself in mission. However, I was not placed in my top three regions."[6] "I was definitely given a choice, but I can see that the choices I made were determined by the opportunities presented to me by the leaders of the organization and church."[7] "I applied for pastoral positions all over the country, but my age and gender seemed to be an obstacle for many churches."[8] "I wanted to go to Thailand, but health issues meant I couldn't go anywhere I wanted, so I ended up serving in Taiwan. Health issues brought us back to Australia."[9] "I had to halt my work in ministry due to having children. There was always an expectation that I would have children from my community, society, and myself. At times the expectation was too much. After children, it was difficult to go back to my ministry role in a paid capacity."[10] "I applied for a ton of pastoral positions at churches all over the country, but I was finally hired by the church I had grown up in."[11]

Interestingly, 78 percent of these women said they were given extensive or significant opportunities to serve in ministry or mission before choosing to go into church-based ministry or serve on the mission field. In addition, 19.5 percent were neutral, and only 2.5 percent said they had not been given opportunities.

5. Research participant thirty-three.
6. Research participant sixteen.
7. Research participant twenty-three.
8. Research participant thirty-two.
9. Research participant thirteen.
10. Research participant twenty-eight.
11. Research participant thirty-two.

Discrimination, Inequalities, Racism, Sexism, and Stereotypes

Our hope in the research was to explore the experiences these women had with discrimination, inequalities, racism, sexism, and stereotypes of Asian women. Many women felt that their gender, ethnicity, and marital status meant they were excluded from leadership roles in the church or mission agencies. Some recounted how they were more qualified and experienced than their husbands, but their husbands were offered many more preaching, teaching, translation, and leadership roles. Others reported how they had many opportunities to lead and teach overseas but were denied these ministries upon returning to Australia. One woman spoke of the numerous opportunities she had for ministry, but those churches expected her to do all these for free because she was an Asian woman. "I felt the injustice. I have been confronting these issues for years. I think diversity is open, but equality is not."[12]

Forty-five percent of the women reported experiencing racism or discrimination in local church ministry or overseas missions, with almost 20 percent saying their experience of these things was constant or significant. Fifty-eight percent of the women reported experiencing sexism in local church ministry or overseas missions, with 33.5 percent saying their experience of sexism was substantial. There were also 44.5 percent of women who spoke of experiencing negative stereotypes of Asian women in local church ministry or overseas mission, with 25 percent saying their experience of these stereotypes was constant or significant. When asked what these stereotypes are, the women offered a variety of answers: an expectation that Asian women will be quiet and submissive; a view that Asian women are reserved in public but bossy, dominant, controlling, irrational, emotional, and competitive at home; comments about their English abilities, even when they grew up in Australia; seeing them as Asians first and persons second; a sexualized and fetishized view of Asian women; a belief that Asian women are domestic and hospitable and naturally good at women and children's ministries; an expectation that Asian women are good at administration, finances,

12. Research participant twenty-four.

and bookkeeping; an idea that Asian women are caring, soft, nurturing, docile, sexually available, submissive, and domestic. These stereotypes weighed heavily on many women, seemed difficult to shake, and impacted their missions, personal lives, and ministries. Some women reported that these stereotypes were perpetuated by Asian men and by patriarchal Asian churches and cultures, but others said these are Western images.

We asked the women if they had experienced more racism and sexism in local church ministry or overseas missions. The breakdown for racism was 25 percent in local ministry and 14 percent in overseas mission, and for sexism, it was 22 percent in local ministry and 19.5 percent in overseas mission. The women felt that racism and sexism were a bigger problem in local church ministry in Australia than in overseas missions.

Did this racism, sexism, or discrimination occur within their Christian organization? Around two-thirds reported that it did. "Sexism is subtle like the women are expected to take minutes for meetings. They are expectation[s] women shouldn't have strong views or that they should respect the men and let them lead."[13] Another woman wrote the following:

> Yes. When I got married, I did not take my husband's surname, but they changed my name when I joined the mission organization. They took my identity and made it something they needed it to be for their convenience. It was disempowering, sexist (why didn't they ask my husband to change his name?), and racist (I wanted to retain my Chinese identity). In Asia, husbands and wives have different surnames, which seemed to be misunderstood by this white Western mission organization. When I first joined my sending organization, I had been in ministry for many years, speaking at conferences, and was a known Bible teacher. But at the interview to join the mission organization, the mission leaders just spoke to my husband the whole time. They ignored me. I was confused, and I asked them, "Does it even matter what my gifts are?" They said, "motherhood is your main

13. Research participant eleven.

ministry." It was dehumanizing. I didn't feel like I had a role to play, and I felt invisible. What if my role is to be a mother but also to do ministry? It was demeaning and made me angry.[14]

Another woman wrote, "There [is] more racism and sexism in local ministry but especially in theological education. Theological education has little interest in what's going on in other cultures and ethnicities. A lot of the senior leaders and committees are just made up of white men and women. Racism is always under the surface. The colleges and seminaries pride themselves on being inclusive, progressive, etc., but racism and sexism are always there."[15]

Christian organizations need to listen closely to the experiences of these women. "When I came into a leadership role, much of the racism increased. Or when others become my leader, their racial biases toward me started to emerge, and they become more resistant to me because of my gender and race. I feel the power dynamics and how they are directed toward me as an Asian woman in the organization, sometimes explicitly and sometimes under the surface."[16] According to one of the women:

> Many of these churches and organizations are the epitome of white privilege. I dread any Diocesan meeting as they tend to be full of well-meaning white people who think they're "woke" but unwittingly keep the status quo going. I've even had some bad racist and sexist encounters with my bishop. The first time I met the bishop, he went on to gleefully tell me about how exciting his experience was in the Philippines (he went to Mindanao) and asked me if I had ever been there. Not to mention the appalling email he sent the diocese about his experiences—he fetishized his experiences there. I don't have words to describe the anger, hurt, and disgust I felt as a Filipino woman reading that letter.[17]

14. Research participant thirty-four.
15. Research participant nineteen.
16. Research participant thirty-five.
17. Research participant five.

Did this racism, sexism, or discrimination occur within Christian leadership or a local church? Around half the women said yes. "It seems it's not okay for some Caucasian leaders to have Asian women (or men) rise in leadership. Caucasians can sometimes be okay when we are serving in ministry, but not when we move into leadership roles. They like it when we do ministry (serving asylum seekers, the poor, the community, etc.) but not when we move into leadership. And being female and Chinese is especially a problem in this regard."[18] "I was told that as a female, I am too emotional and can't make good decisions."[19] A couple of the women commented on the problems that reside in progressive leadership circles. "The progressives can be some of the most fundamentalist and least willing to admit their own racism etc."[20] "Gender stereotyping does occur within my local church. I would consider that a racial microaggression which is systemic racism."[21]

These women also spoke of their experiences of racism, sexism, and discrimination within local communities while on the mission field. Some spoke of racism in some Asian cultures and the expectations that they should have fairer skin and better local language abilities. Some of the women who are married to white men spoke of their husbands' special treatment, which was denied to them.

What impact does this racism, sexism, or discrimination have on these women? Some say they have adapted to it over time, others say it has made them stronger and more determined, others talk about suppressing or denying their gifts to accommodate these realities. Others talk about the deep hurt they carry. Churches, denominations, and mission agencies need to listen to the experiences of these women. "I feel discouraged. I'm a strong advocate, raising questions of advocacy, etc. There are situations where I speak up and are shut down. Universities and schools respect the diversity of opinion, in contrast to many Christian organizations."[22] "I felt

18. Research participant twenty.
19. Research participant nine.
20. Research participant thirty-five.
21. Research participant two.
22. Research participant thirteen.

inferior. Comments such as 'you're a good girl'—just for doing my job, whereas I never heard comments like that for my equivalent male leaders. It made me question whether I have the actual authority or power to change things, or do I just make an organization look good because I'm a female Asian leader? It can feel tokenistic, and I feel I may not have any actual power to change structures and systems."[23] "I find the male dominance in the church frustrating—it is like Australia might have been pre-1960s. It makes me feel like I don't have a voice, and I'm unimportant."[24] "Sometimes it made me resistant to working with those groups again and would often leave a bitter taste towards the overall leadership for not addressing such issues."[25] "It made me want to quit and leave the church altogether."[26] "It was a massive burden to fit gender expectations of Chinese culture and Reformed culture. I struggled a lot with the expectations on me and resented them. But I had no safe person to talk to about them, except for my husband. Racism has been less of a problem, given we don't see our denominational leaders much. Still, there have been a couple of instances of racial/gender ignorance from our Anglo senior leader, which makes it hard for me to trust him."[27] "I would second guess myself and be more conservative in my decisions. I knew making bad choices would be held against me as an Asian woman, and making waves wasn't going to be perceived well."[28] "Initially, it made me angry and more determined to prove the stereotypes wrong. But over time, it becomes more exhausting than anything else."[29]

We also asked these women if, in their experience, Asian Australian women are neglected in the study of missions (local or global). Around 80 percent of the women said yes. They are aware of the extent of ministry and mission that Asian women do in Australia

23. Research participant twelve.
24. Research participant thirty-six.
25. Research participant thirty.
26. Research participant twenty-six.
27. Research participant twenty-eight.
28. Research participant twenty-nine.
29. Research participant thirty-two.

and overseas and how this goes unreported. They often feel ignored or invisible. One woman wrote, "This is a neglected area of study. God has used me very powerfully in mission (and others), but this isn't always recognized. When I was getting my book published (as an Asian scholar), I was told by the publisher that they want to publish books about Asian Christianity (writing from the outside), not books written by Asian scholars written from the inside."[30] "Yes! I think due to the lack of leadership opportunities, the experiences of Asian Australian women in missions are not necessarily voiced by them—their male counterparts or leaders represent them."[31] "So, few Asian women are even taken seriously on a scholarship level, and the study of missions is still a white man's field."[32] "I think in many ways Asian people, in general, are neglected by Western society. There's still a sense of otherness and lack of information. I think Westerners are still somewhat afraid of Asian people, and this carries over into Christian circles and the study of missions as well."[33]

Almost 75 percent of the women said they are overlooked for leadership opportunities in mission and ministry because of their gender and ethnicity. "I think the stereotype of Asian women as submissive and domestic means that they are often not looked upon as viable candidates for leadership. I also think that the needs of Asian communities go unnoticed by most churches, and so they don't see the need for Asian representation in leadership."[34]

Experiences of Inequality, Powerlessness, Vulnerability, and Woundedness in Mission and Ministry

Most of the women (around 95 percent) recounted stories and experiences of inequality, powerlessness, vulnerability, and woundedness. Some of this was within churches and mission agencies, and some within the cultures they were serving. These experiences

---

30. Research participant nineteen.
31. Research participant twenty-three.
32. Research participant thirty.
33. Research participant thirty-two.
34. Research participant thirty-two.

included being disregarded as a minority voice, treated differently as a "model minority," treated like a frail Asian woman, and having church, society, and patriarchal systems marginalize them. Many reported the difficulties of being "overlooked, not taken seriously, misunderstood, joked about,"[35] and even sexualized. One woman wrote, "When I was first hired, a family left the church because they couldn't accept a female pastor. They thought I would serve as a sexual temptation to the men on my team."[36]

One woman described how Asian Australian women in her church and Christian leadership are often sexually harassed by Christian men and sometimes by Christian male leaders. She explained how Christian organizations did not take the complaints of these women seriously. She also described how these women take measures to protect themselves and not appear attractive to men. In her experience, the sexualization of Asian women in Western cultures is also a problem in the church. Churches have been too slow to address this problem.

Many churches and Christian organizations are led and controlled by white men. This offers up significant challenges. One of the women lamented:

> I have an all-white board, with more than half being white males over fifty years old. Our partner organization representatives are also all white. But this is not a reflection of the diversity of the people we serve. I have felt that the power structures have discouraged me from working toward change. It's hard to change things when you're the only person of color in the room, and when you hear negative comments to do with race and power ... I need more diversity to affirm my own experience—or it just feels lonely in ministry. I have felt it's all okay when you are at the beginning of the ministry, and many people support you. But as you go higher up the ranks, I'm not sure if I have the authority and power actually to change things.[37]

---

35. Research participant thirty-one.
36. Research participant thirty-two.
37. Research participant fourteen.

Some of these women felt excluded from white culture and other "people of color." "I have heard many Asian women—including myself—express frustration that Asians are excluded from the push to give people of color more power. White people see us as the "model minority" who do not share the experience of Latinx or Black people, and other people of color sometimes see Asians as too privileged to understand their oppression."[38]

Some of these women spoke of a "triple marginalization" experienced through racism, sexism, and damaging church cultures and stereotypes. For example:

> I experience triple marginalization in my local church, wider Anglo society, and being a woman . . . For me, this has mainly been in microaggressions: stereotypes and expectations of what I'm meant to do or be like. It has also meant initially not doing what I think I'm gifted at (preaching, strategic planning). Instead, churches require me to do women's, children's, and care ministries, which my community needs. Funnily enough, my husband, who is the pastor, is asked to be that manager and director, which he hates. We have often wanted to swap roles as he is much better domestically than I. Of course, we can never say that out loud to others.[39]

The gifts and abilities of these women were often limited or criticized. This is particularly true for those serving in Reformed and Evangelical circles. One woman told this story of an experience while serving in a university ministry.

> I was working with international students at a university campus and tried to explain the song "How Great Thou Art?" The leaders told me off for preaching and teaching. I was told to share my testimony but not share the gospel because when I do that, it is a "woman preaching." This felt demeaning and limiting. I shouldn't need to justify sharing Jesus with people—but that's often the case in Australia. My gender has dictated the gospel going out

---

38. Research participant fifteen.
39. Research participant twenty-eight.

from my lips. In my experience, that doesn't happen on the mission field, but it does in Australia.[40]

How do inequality and marginalization make these women feel? Many reported feeling frustrated, angry, hurt, unvalued, inferior, isolated, lonely, afraid, annoyed, indignant, silenced, powerless, exploited, second class, discouraged, discriminated against, treated unjustly, and sad. They also spoke of their efforts to work through these feelings and experiences, trust God, learn forgiveness, and confront the systems and power structures whenever possible. "It all makes me feel inferior or not important. But in the meantime, I want to avoid the temptation to self-pity, even while we address these underlying issues. The change needs to come from the inside, not just the voices from the margins."[41] "I feel injustice and discouraged. I openly discuss and confront the issue. I educate people with patience."[42]

Challenges and Benefits of Being an Asian Australian Woman in Ministry and Mission

It would be a mistake, however, to put all the emphasis on inequality and difficulties. These women do not see themselves as victims and would not want us to portray them in that way. There are many opportunities for Asian Australian women in missions and ministry, and their contributions are immense. Their ability to understand and traverse multiple cultures and societies is just one example of the gifts and contributions Asian Australian women bring to Christian service, ministry, and mission.

We invited the women to reflect on the challenges and benefits of being a woman of Asian ethnic descent in ministry and mission. It is worth noting that more of these women said that being an Asian woman in ministry and mission is an advantage (88.89 percent) rather than a liability (25 percent).

---

40. Research participant thirteen.
41. Research participant nineteen.
42. Research participant twenty-four.

We start with the difficulties and challenges. Of the thirty-six surveys conducted over sixty minutes, here are the ten most common problems named (for local church ministry and global missions): fewer leadership opportunities (36.11 percent); the expectation of filing roles that are not my gifting (55.56 percent); difficult communication in teams (47.22 percent); not being able to use gifts of teaching and preaching (41.67 percent); not being respected within society (25 percent); not feeling safe and protected (22.22 percent); sexual harassment or assault (8.33 percent); lack of support or accountability (38.89 percent); not considered an Australian, but only Asian (41.67 percent); standing out as different (47.22 percent). Some of the other difficulties named in the interviews include a lack of female Asian Christian leader role models and limited opportunities because of stereotypes about Asian women and their gifts. One woman said:

> I feel like I'm not always considered when forming a leadership team. I feel like I'm on the fringe and observing what is going on in the church. I also have a speaking gift but was given administrative tasks and bookkeeping (so stereotypes come into play). I am a people person but not always perceived that way because of stereotypes. Sometimes my communication style is seen as too blunt. Asian and Australian culture is different in terms of communication styles. (I stand out as different, but I feel very comfortable and confident with being different—a positive.) Chinese feel I'm too Australian and Australians see me as Asian. But this can be a positive, as Australians see me as a bridge to understanding Asians (and vice versa). Sometimes Asian women are treated in a flirtatious way (so I don't always feel safe).[43]

Of these women, 68.75 percent said they faced sexism, racism, and discrimination in local church ministry in Australia, and only 31.25 percent said they experienced these things in overseas missions. "In Australia, the roles that a woman can take on are very restrictive in some church settings. But as a missionary, you can do everything and anything. Some of my experience has been shaped

---

43. Research participant eighteen.

by the conservative Sydney church scene (and Sydney Chinese churches). Being in overseas missions leads you to work across theological, cultural, and denominational differences."[44]

When asked if these difficulties have changed in Australia over the last couple of decades, 35.48 percent said yes, 32.26 percent said no, and 32.26 percent were unsure. The picture seems to be mixed. Attitudes are changing in many parts of Australian society, but parts of the church remain resistant to change on cultural and gender issues. "There [is] growing openness and integration and talk about culture and ethnicity. There is much more openness in Australian society. There is a lot of talk about cultural competence, but I often wonder if people understand what cultural competency involves. It often feels like: 'We welcome you, but don't touch power or leadership or money.' Also, people talk about cultural inclusion, but they may complain about bilingual worship or translation."[45] There are, however, some encouraging signs. "More people have become interested in what ethnic minorities and women have to say in the past couple of years. There are more opportunities to speak and be heard and to be invited to a seat at the table."[46]

As noted previously, 88.89 percent of the Asian Australian Christian women surveyed and interviewed said that being an Asian woman in ministry and mission is advantageous, with 50 percent saying that the benefits are "abundant," and 38.89 percent saying they are "significant."

Of the thirty-six surveys conducted over sixty minutes, here are the ten most common advantages named (for local church ministry and global missions): acceptance within society (44.44 percent); not considered a threat (72.22 percent); ability to connect with a variety of cultures (97.22 percent); Australians are usually loved around the world (30.56 percent); don't stand out as different on the mission field (33.33 percent); ability to work alongside a specific people group that interests me (58.33 percent); opportunities to be trusted with children (61.11 percent); opportunities

---

44. Research participant seven.
45. Research participant twenty.
46. Research participant twenty-nine.

in leadership (44.44 percent); offered protection and honor (27.78 percent); identification with those who are vulnerable in society (72.22 percent). There is so much to unpack here, including the ability to work across cultures, the ability not to be perceived as a threat (the way a white male might be), and the ability to identify with and relate to the most vulnerable people in a society. In some cultures, people assume that Asian women understand the importance of family values, hospitality, collective and communal mentalities, and mentoring women and children. These are all advantages for Asian women in mission. These women also talked about being perceived as intelligent, caring, reliable, diligent, thoughtful, and competent.

One Asian Australian woman wrote the following of her experience in the mission field.

> People don't feel like I have an agenda just by looking at me. There are not many Asian missionaries locally, so they don't feel like I'm just here to convert them. I can invite people to my home in a way that is harder for white men to do. I can invite them to a group or personal meeting, and there are no worries about agendas. It is easier to connect with teenagers and with elders as well. The guard is a lot lower when I approach them. Being an Asian means that other Asians let me know their thoughts very openly. The people I'm trying to reach would share their true thoughts with me, whereas they may not share with a white Australian. I also feel like I'm welcomed by other immigrant groups (like the African community). People who feel vulnerable identify with me (especially migrants) because they feel like I can relate to them and understand them. And being Asian means I don't stand out but can blend in and serve among them.[47]

Another woman reflected on her work with refugees and asylum seekers and how her ethnicity and gender were advantageous. "I was able to work in a detention camp on Manus Island for a while, and the asylum seekers were more open and comfortable with me than with white people."[48]

47. Research participant nineteen.
48. Research participant twenty-one.

A couple of the women also reflected on the fact that "Asians are coming more to the center of the cultural and world stage"[49] and that the "wider Western Christian world is more open in recent years to minority voices."[50] While this research has reflected on the difficulties and inequalities faced by Asian women in ministry and mission, the advantages of being an Asian woman in these contexts are also abundant.

Theological, Ecclesiological, and Missiological Challenges

What theological themes create problems for women in ministry and mission who have Asian ethnic backgrounds? These may include ecclesiology, missiology, a theology of sex and gender, or other theological views and constructs. The women surveyed and interviewed responded to this question by naming complementarian, colonizing, and patriarchal theologies. Almost three-quarters said that strict gender roles, patriarchal structures, and complementarian theologies were the most considerable problems. These things are the most likely to prevent them from serving fully in mission and ministry.

While the women recognized that gender roles and patriarchal systems are present in many Asian cultures, some expressed concern that complementarian theologies are a Western import that negatively impacts Asian Christianity and women in ministry and mission. "Westerners are importing movements into the urban Asian church, like complementarian theology (which is very different from the more indigenous movements)."[51]

The tendency for mission agencies to place people in contexts based on their ethnicity also caused problems. "You can be forced to serve in a country or a ministry specifically targeted at your racial background. However, God may not have placed it in your heart to

---

49. Research participant six.
50. Research participant twenty-eight.
51. Research participant nineteen.

serve in those ministries."⁵² "Some mission agencies prioritize those of a similar ethnicity (over other ethnicities in the context)."⁵³

A few women reflected on their white Western ethnic superiority experiences and the theological ideas and images that supported this problem.

> When children are taught about the church, they still tend to be shown images of white disciples and a white Jesus. Western theological training also tends to idealize the buoyant leader who is loud and able to get a crowd worked up about a cause. Some Asian women fit this description; others don't. This may be because we were raised in very different cultures. (Or they are, in fact, this type of leader, but their audience doesn't see them this way because they're Asian.) Asian women can also have a hard time fitting into progressive spaces, such as LGBTQ supportive Christian groups since what's considered popular in these communities is still a pretty white ideal.⁵⁴

One woman wrote of her conviction that white superiority is still embedded in church, mission, and society.

> The idea of us all being made equal in the image of Christ is difficult for me to live into. I do not feel like I can be my whole self in the places I serve or worship, but I feel like my work is important. I wonder if the cost for Asian women in largely white denominations is worth it. We do so much more emotional and spiritual labor, but we are also expected to hide the pain. I don't know if hiding the pain is "honor culture" or if it's the larger cultural pressure to hide the pain and the true nature of racism and sexism.⁵⁵

---

52. Research participant twelve.
53. Research participant ten.
54. Research participant seventeen.
55. Research participant eight.

White superiority can relate to fear and suspicion of Asian cultures, patriarchal theologies, and dominant Christian leadership images.

A belief in strict gender roles holds women back from ministry. Women who refuse to abide by those roles are feared and rejected. Add to that the fear and suspicion that Westerners already hold toward Asian people, and you can see why Asian women don't get much representation in church leadership. Many churches don't even teach that the Savior they worship is an Asian man. Persistent media representation of biblical characters as white Westerners hasn't helped at all.[56]

Women in the surveys and interviews named other challenges. These include theological ideas about submission to elders, harmful theologies of manhood and womanhood, and "negative views of charismatic leaders (a lot of Asian Christianity is very charismatic, so this is a problem)."[57]

BEING ASIAN AND FEMALE IN A WHITE MALE GOD'S CHURCH AND WORLD

The stories of these Asian Australian women reveal the vastness of their contribution to missions and ministry. Their testimonies also show the breadth of their exposure to discrimination, sexism, racism, stereotyping, objectification, and mistreatment in church and society. They told of their negative experiences of the powers and principalities at work in religious institutions and the world. They expressed their sense of vulnerability and marginalization. They recounted their awareness of inequalities and injustices. These problematic experiences span a wide range of Australian Christian organizations. These Christian groups include churches, mission agencies, theological colleges, denominational networks, charities, conferences, non-profits, and more.

56. Research participant four.
57. Research participant one.

The findings of our research replicate similar studies in Christian settings in the United States. Christian organizations must do better if they desire to display the justice and gospel of Jesus Christ and the values of God's kingdom.

In 2008, Christina L. Kima, Tamara L. Anderson, M. Elizabeth Lewis Hall, and Michele M. Willingham published a phenomenological study examining the discrimination experiences of Asian American female faculty at North American Christian universities. Their article is titled "Asian and Female in the White God's World."[58] Ten of the eleven women interviewed recounted mistreatment and discrimination based on race and gender. Three distinct themes emerged in this study. First, the lack of diversity among faculty, students, and administrators on campuses. Second, the existence of naivete and denial toward the presence of racism, sexism, and discrimination on Christian campuses and in syllabi, promotions, policies, and so on. These academics and their institutions often justified this, emphasizing unity, harmony, and a colorblind ideal. "Love had become a rationale to ignore differences and invalidate hurts."[59] Third, a "missionary mentality" in the Christian subculture sees Asians, Africans, Middle Easterners, Indigenous peoples, and Latin Americans (anyone who isn't white) as foreign, less capable, and needing Westernization and education. The research among Asian American female faculty of North American Christian universities conducted by Kima, Anderson, Hall, and Willingham, reveals many of the same themes that we found in our research among Asian Australian Christian women in ministry and mission. In conclusion, these North American researchers write:

> The participants' experiences suggest that theological concepts ("love of others") and specific ways of relating to other cultures ("missionary mentality") may be characteristics of the evangelical worldview that are an obstacle to acknowledging discrimination . . . Understanding the particular contexts that contribute to discrimination is essential to addressing the problem . . . Emerson and Smith (2001) began their landmark book, "Divided by

58. Kim et al., "Asian and Female."
59. Kim et al., "Asian and Female," 461.

Faith: Evangelical Religion and the Problem of Race in America" by stating, "This book is a story of how well-intentioned people, their values, and their institutions actually recreate racial divisions and inequalities they ostensibly oppose" (p. 1). The irony of the evangelical worldview is that elements contributing to discrimination are held simultaneously with beliefs that affirm the equality of all people and the principles of justice and love. However, embedded in this contradiction is also hope, as the evangelical worldview contains resources and the moral force to challenge discrimination—resources which should be investigated and empirically examined in pursuit of [Christian academic and other] environments where women of color can thrive.[60]

Asian hate crimes and discriminations against the Asian diaspora have increased during the coronavirus pandemic. One April 2021 survey of Covid-19 related racism against Asian Australians recorded 178 incidents in two weeks (12 incidents per day). That number only includes those that were reported. Most of these racist incidents were committed against women (62 percent) and by strangers (86.5 percent). According to the survey:

> Just over 60 percent of the self-reported incidents included racial slurs, 21 percent included verbal threats, and 15 percent included physical intimidation such as being punched or shoved. Over a third occurred on a public street, 23 percent occurred in supermarkets, 15 percent on public transport, 12 percent in shopping centers, and 11 percent in public parks and community areas... Only 5.6 percent of those surveyed reported their incidents to police.[61]

On March 16, 2021, a twenty-one-year-old white male went on a shooting spree at three spas in Atlanta, Georgia, killing eight people, including six Asian women. This man explained his actions as being motivated by sexual addictions that warred against his

---

60. Kim et al., "Asian and Female," 463. See Emerson and Smith, *Divided by Faith*, 1.

61. Zhou, "Survey of Covid-19 Racism."

Christian convictions—blaming the Asian women for his sexual temptation and addiction and subsequent violence.

Flora x. Tang declares that such North American hate crimes reveal the depth of sexualization and objectification of Asian and other women of color in Western societies. Flora could direct the same concerns to the Australian community and church. She says it's due time we reckoned:

> ... with the harmful, and even deadly, theologies of sexual shame and objectification that permeate our Christian moral imagination. It means refusing to allow women to be blamed as "stumbling blocks" for male sexual sin. It means committing to new practices and catechesis that affirm the inherent goodness of the human body. It means re-examining the ways we speak of sexuality in our own church spaces and redirecting these conversations so that sexual desire is distinguished from sexual violence. "Lead us not into temptation," we must pray. But the temptation from which we must be delivered is not the bodies of vulnerable Asian women. Rather, we are called to resist the temptation to reduce Asian women and other women of color to disembodied objects of male desire. We are called to resist the temptation to falsely direct blame for the Covid-19 pandemic onto our Asian American [or Asian Australian] brothers and sisters, as well as the temptation to continue treating Asian Americans [or Asian Australians] in this country as a perpetual other.[62]

The Atlanta shootings and coronavirus-related hate crimes are a symptom of a broader epidemic. We're talking about an epidemic of sexism, sexualization, racism, "othering," and discrimination against minoritized peoples, and especially minoritized women.[63] Gender and racial microaggressions, discrimination, stereotyping, and sexualization are present within Australian Christian churches and organizations and damage Asian Australian women. Such realities work against the contributions of Asian Australian women and

---

62. Tang, "Lead Us Not," 10. See Hesse, "Race, Class and Gender."
63. Robinson, "Mail-Order Brides."

prevent the church from experiencing the fullness of the gifts of the Spirit poured out on all peoples. Researchers of the University of Maryland developed the Gendered Racial Microaggressions Scale for Asian American Women (GRMSAAW) using data collected from 564 Asian American Women (AAW). The GRMSAAW is significant for assessing "the unique gendered racial microaggressions Asian American women experience and found promising initial psychometric properties measurement utility. Gendered racial microaggressions were significantly associated with Asian American women's depressive symptoms over and above perceived racial microaggressions or sexist events."[64] In other words, gendered racial microaggressions can be demonstrably linked to poor mental health outcomes from Asian American women, and most likely, for other Asian women in the diaspora.

Yet, somehow, in the face of such adversity, Asian Australian women continue to persevere and contribute while compelled to develop coping mechanisms to deal with these realities. Delma Ramos and Varaxy Yi challenge us to move from a deficit to an assets model, paying attention to the coping and system-confronting resources developed by women of color. These women "overcome oppression and marginalization [through] . . . long-term goals and aspirations, awareness of interlocking systems of oppression shaping their experiences . . . commitment to empowering their communities through education, and the support they find within their personal [and professional] networks."[65] Many Asian Australian women respond to hardship, discrimination, and pain with determination and grit. They act to make the church and world a more just and equal place for other marginalized groups. They also confront the systems and structures that perpetuate gendered racial stereotypes, injustices, and oppression.

---

64. Keum et al., "Gendered Racial Microaggressions Scale."

65. Ramos and Yi, "Doctoral Women of Color," 135. For an interesting study of how racial and gender stereotypes shape the lives and limit the educational and professional possibilities of Asian Australian women, see Matthews, "Racialised Schooling."

Sunburnt Country, Sweeping Pains

ADDRESSING STEREOTYPES AND SYSTEMIC OPPRESSION

The Asian Australian women in our research described struggling with stereotypes and the systemic oppression and discrimination these stereotypes represent and perpetuate.[66] In *More Than Serving Tea: Asian American Women on Expectations, Relationships, Leadership and Faith*, six Asian American women tackle these stereotypes head-on (these women are Nikki A. Toyama-Szeto, Tracey Gee, Kathy Khang, Christie Heller de Leon, Asifa Dean, and Jeanette Yep).[67] They show how diaspora Asian women are often caught between two worlds, with each presenting restricting cultural and gender stereotypes and prescribed roles. The good news of Jesus Christ challenges these stereotypes, confronting how these stereotypes sexualize, objectify, restrain, and devalue diaspora Asian women. Instead, God desires to work through their ethnic and gender identities, freeing them to explore their ministry and leadership gifts fully.

What follows is a fascinating conversation between Rachel Held Evans, Kathy Khang, and Nikki Toyama-Szeto on cultural stereotypes and the diverse nature of Asian American and Asian Australian populations and churches.[68] Note the stereotypes diaspora Asian women face and the insults, exclusions, and microaggressions. Pay attention to the diversity and complexity of the Asian diaspora and the expectations placed on immigrant populations to assimilate and step out of their cultural comfort zones—expectations not placed on White Christians.

> *Rachel Held Evans*: "In More Than Serving Tea, you two join four other Asian American women to explore how family expectations and cultural stereotypes often assume that Asian American women can only fill rigidly defined roles. Can you share a little of how you have experienced that in your life? What's the 'good news' for Asian American women who feel frustrated or burdened by these expectations?"

---

66. For a useful article on addressing Asian stereotypes in Western education, see Patel and Crocco, "Teaching About South Asian Women."
67. Toyama-Szeto and Gee, *More Than Serving Tea*.
68. Evans, "More Than Serving Tea."

Sweeping Pains

Nikki Toyama-Szeto: "Most of my interactions with cultural stereotypes have assumed that because I'm an Asian woman, I could be either a dragon lady, a newscaster, or a demure sexualized object. Those are the portrayals of AA women. Today we have more diverse pictures. But it's the small comments of, 'your English is so good' and 'where are you from?' that communicate that you're an outsider or that you don't belong. I was born in Chicago, and I'm a fourth-generation American, but still, I will receive these questions that my friend, a recent immigrant from Poland, never will receive."

Rachel Held Evans: "Christians love to talk about how faith is changing in the U.S., and we often point to statistics that paint a gloomy picture of church attendance and religious involvement. We also have a bad habit of ignoring the continued growth of Christianity among immigrant and ethnic minority communities in the U.S. What's something you wish more people knew about Asian American Christians? What are some common mistakes we make in discussing multiethnic Christianity?"

Nikki Toyama-Szeto: "I wish that people knew that Asian American Christianity is not a monolith—but a diverse group of creative and committed followers of Christ. Asian American churches come in many shapes and sizes and span the theological spectrum. They might be some of the best places to go to learn about powerful prayer, costly discipleship, death to self, community life. I think there are lots of different values that God holds dear that are being expressed in the life of our Asian American churches. Asian American Christians are usually bicultural—we must be, to function in both our families and broader American society. And I think that's something that the American church can receive from the Asian American church."

Kathy Khang: "I would say that even in your question, Rachel, you make a common mistake. I was late to the emergent/emerging church conversations because Christians who loved the talk about how faith is and continues to change in the U.S. were and continue to be predominantly White. 'We' can mean different groups of people in different contexts, and honestly, I often have to point out that the 'we' too often excludes non-White voices at the table. Those gloomy statistics are gloomy if you are a White church in a White-lead religious movement. Diversity and multiethnicity are then, at their worst, seen as a threat to the 'way it was,' a gilded memory of a Christian and secular history that has been documented and repeated through White dominant culture's lens and messengers. If 'we' want to discuss multiethnicity, we all need to know our cultural lenses. That is where the White Church may have some good work ahead in understanding its own culture, preferences, and strengths as well as differences within the White, dominant cultural experience...

"The Asian American Christian church is extremely diverse, vibrant, multigenerational, and cutting edge with all the struggles and concerns of the historically White Church—evangelical and mainline. I wish more people understood that 'Asian American' includes Thai, Hmong, Laotian, Vietnamese, Pilipino, Pakistani, Indian, Pacific Islander, Chinese, Japanese, and Korean. Our cultures are not all the same. There are nuances to shared values and distinct differences, and that plays out in the beautiful, diverse expressions of our faith and faith practices.

> "And that goes back to the discussions about multiethnicity. There is a cost for a hyphenated American like me to help what once was a White church become multiethnic. I have to leave my immigrant church, a concern for first-generation congregations who saw and still see churches as both a strategy and physical space to connect generations divided by language, education, power, and levels of assimilation through faith. I'd love to see more conversations about the cost of asking English-speaking second-generation Asian Americans to leave their comfortable, homogenous Asian American churches without offering up a similar call to the White church."

Stereotypes are linked to systemic and structural oppression and discrimination not necessarily because they are wrong but because they serve an (often painful and repressive) regulatory function. In an article called "What's Wrong with Stereotypes?" Erin Beeghly points out that focusing on the falsity of a stereotype isn't the most helpful way of showing how stereotypes oppress and damage people.

Sweeping Pains

> Stereotypes are commonly alleged to be false or inaccurate views of groups. For shorthand, I call this the *falsity hypothesis*. The falsity hypothesis is widespread and is often one of the first reasons people cite when they explain why we shouldn't use stereotypic views in cognition, reasoning, or speech . . . I argue against the falsity hypothesis on both empirical and ameliorative grounds. In its place, I sketch a more promising view of stereotypes—which avoids the falsity hypothesis . . . Stereotypes are controlling images or ideas that enjoy both a psychological and cultural existence, which serve a regulative social function.[69]

Stereotypes, whether or not they contain accuracies, serve to maintain group hierarchies, facilitate oppression, regulate society and institutions, control images and ideas, categorize individuals, and shape perceptions of ourselves and others. Therefore, stereotypes can be emotionally laden and socially oppressive and serve to regulate "what is permissible, normal, or appropriate in a given context, for particular kinds of people."[70] That's what is wrong with stereotypes.

Qi Wang says that the good news is that conscious and implicit stereotypes can be challenged and corrected. But this requires collective and intentional effort. Wang writes:

> Ultimately, unwinding racism is a long-term, collaborative effort that must take place at the societal and cultural level and begin with children before they have formed negative stereotypes of Asians and other groups . . . Asian individuals and communities also need to more actively promote our cultures and facilitate intergroup understanding. Of course, that applies to *all* groups in a diverse and multicultural society . . . Intergroup understanding and acceptance are critical for building a harmonious society.[71]

The same is true for the church and other Christian organizations.

---

69. Beeghly, "What's Wrong with Stereotypes?," 33.
70. Beeghly, "What's Wrong with Stereotypes?," 54.
71. Massari, "Racism On Her Mind."

FACING THE RACIST AND SEXIST CURRENTS OF THE GREAT WHITE FLOOD

Racism and sexism are prevalent in Australian culture. Church and society need to face this reality with honesty, sorrow, a listening ear to those who suffer, and commitment to change. Australian Christians must repent and ask for forgiveness for their complicity. Aboriginal and Torres Strait Islanders, immigrant groups, people of non-mainstream sexualities and genders, and women and girls have especially undergone racism, bigotry, discrimination, and sexism in this country.

The Australian Equal Rights Alliance report that one-third of Australian women have experienced violence and sexual harassment since the age of fifteen. Women are more likely to live below the poverty line. Women make up 32 percent of Parliamentarians. Women spend twice as much time on unpaid work as men.[72]

Australians Together and other groups describe how Indigenous Australians experience shorter life expectancies, higher rates of infant mortality, poorer health, and lower levels of education and employment.[73] One Victorian study found:

> Indigenous Victorian adults were four times more likely than their non-Indigenous counterparts to have experienced racism in the preceding 12 months; odds ratio (OR) = 4.3 (95 percent confidence interval (CI): 3.2–5.8) ... When the non-Indigenous comparison group consisted of adults of mainly Anglo-Celtic origin, Indigenous adults were seven times more likely (OR = 7.2; 5.3–9.7) to have experienced racism ... We argue that a human rights-based approach to policy-making for the elimination of systemic and interpersonal racism offers an opportunity and viable alternative to current policy-making that continues to be dominated by a paternalistic approach that reinforces racism and the resulting inequities.[74]

---

72. Equality Rights Alliance, "Gender Equality in Australia."
73. Australians Together, "Indigenous Disadvantage in Australia."
74. Markwick et al., "Experiences of Racism."

Researchers at the University of Western Sydney have launched an initiative called the Challenging Racism Project. Their research measured the extent and forms of racist attitudes and experiences in Australia. This study was profiled by SBS television for a documentary entitled "Is Australia Racist?" which was first aired on February 26th, 2017. The research was extensive, peer-reviewed, and representative of the Australian population. While it found a broad desire among Australians for cultural diversity and anti-racism initiatives, it also found the following evidence of racism within Australian society.

> High levels of antipathy were found towards various groups of Australians.
>
> - 27.6 percent of respondents indicated they would be "extremely" or "very concerned" if a relative were to marry a Muslim. In total, 63 per cent of respondents expressed some degree (ranging from slightly-extremely) of intolerance/discomfort with Muslim Australians.
> - 51.4 percent expressed anti-Middle Eastern sentiment.
> - 43.9 percent of respondents expressed anti-African sentiment.
> - Most Australians recognize that racism exists within Australia (79.3 percent).
>
> Experiences of racism amongst the respondents were quite high:
>
> - 34.8 percent of participants had experienced racism on public transport or in the street.
> - 32.8 percent of participants had experienced racism in the workplace.
>
> 32.8 percent of participants had experienced racism within an educational institution.[75]

---

75. Western Sydney University, "Face Up to Racism." See the Challenging Racism Project website at https://www.westernsydney.edu.au/challengingracism/challenging_racism_project.

Critical books for understanding racism in Australia include Anne Pattel-Gray's *The Great White Flood*, Amanuel Elias, Fethi Mansouri, and Yin Paradies's *Racism in Australia Today*, and David Hollinsworth's *Race and Racism in Australia*. Other books include Stan Grant's *Australia Day*, *The Australian Dream*, and *Talking to My Country*, Derek Reilly's *Gulpilil*, Thomas Mayor's *Finding the Heart of the Nation*, Sarah Maddison's *The Colonial Fantasy*, Chloe Hooper's *The Tall Man*, and Schultz and Phillip's *First Things First*.[76] Every Australian should read the *Uluru Statement from the Heart*.[77] Australia needs a "Makarrata Commission" (described in the Uluru Statement as a way to "supervise a process of agreement-making between governments and First Nations and truth-telling about our history"). We also recommend that every Australian support Common Grace and their Aboriginal and Torres Strait Islander justice initiatives. Common Grace offers a wide range of resources for reconciliation and Aboriginal justice.[78] Aside from Aboriginal and Torres Strait Islander justice initiatives, Common Grace also offers resources on creation and climate justice, asylum seeker and refugee justice, and domestic and family violence justice.

Asian Australian women are too often swept up in the racist and sexist currents of, as Anne Pattel-Gray and Lyndel Robb put it, "the great white flood." Like Aboriginal peoples and other marginalized groups, these women suffer from past and present racist and sexist attitudes, systems, and social structures. Anne Pattel-Gray writes, "In 1770, James Cook wrote in his Journal, 'from what I have seen in the Natives of New Holland they may appear to some to be the most wretched People on Earth.' On this racist lie was built modern Australian society. For over 200 years, the Australian social structure has contributed to racism and, amazingly, continues such actions today."[79]

76. Grant, *Australia Day*; *Talking to My Country*; *Australian Dream*; Rielly, *Gulpilil*; Mayor, *Heart of the Nation*; Maddison, *Colonial Fantasy*; Hooper, *Tall Man*; Schultz and Phillips, *First Things First*; Pattel-Gray, *Great White Flood*; Elias et al., *Racism in Australia Today*; Hollinsworth, *Race and Racism*.

77. Uluru Statement, "Uluru Statement from the Heart."

78. Common Grace, "Aboriginal and Torres Strait Islander Justice."

79. Pattel-Gray, *Great White Flood*, 15.

DEVELOPING A THEOLOGY OF JUSTICE, MARGINALITY, AND INTERSECTIONALITY

The church can't respond adequately to the stories and experiences of Asian Australian women without a theology of justice, marginality, and intersectionality. These three themes interweave. Justice is required to address the experiences of marginalized people and the systems, powers, and principalities at work. All people need justice, especially those mistreated, marginalized, silenced, and overlooked because of intersectional veracities. Marginality often occurs because of injustices, intersectional realities, and discriminations. Intersectionality reveals the complexity and pervasiveness of marginality and injustice. Developing an adequate theology of justice, marginality, and intersectionality is deep work. Such work takes considerable time, repentance, and self-reflection.

Justice

A biblical theology of justice compels us to honor those marginalized and mistreated. The Spirit of God calls us to serve, welcome, and respect these people in the humility and love that Jesus modeled. In *Healing Our Broken Humanity*, Grace Ji-Sun Kim and Graham write:

> God is a just God who hates injustice. Injustice is a contagious sin that breaks and angers the heart of God. God's antidote to injustice is truth, love, grace, reconciliation, peace, compassion, and welcome.

God calls the church to be a just church. Our vocation is to be a just community that pursues justice for all peoples and all creation, by acting justly, loving mercy, and walking humbly with our God . . .

We must not be silent in the face of poverty, exploitation, injustice, sexism, racism, misogyny, torture, hate, division, conflict, authoritarianism, etc. We must choose to speak and act, even when we know we will suffer the consequences. This means speaking out on "Black Lives Matter," poverty, climate change, war, consumption and consumerism, health issues, nuclear weapons, the Palestine/Israel conflict, white privilege, sexism, racism, systemic and structural evils, and more...

Silence speaks volumes. When you or I choose not to act, we are taking a form of action. We witness to Jesus and his kingdom, in our life together, and our risky, prophetic, and just words and actions.

Restoring justice involves prioritizing the wellbeing and human flourishing of the poor, wronged, marginalized, and disadvantaged. This only happens when we prioritize and value their agency and voice and redistribute power and resources.

> Restoring justice is, fundamentally, about following a just God and being a just church. God hates injustice. God is just. The biblical story is one of a just and loving God reaching out to humanity to restore justice, wholeness, healing, and redemption. The church is an alternative community. God calls this church to embrace, proclaim, embody, and practice restored justice. We do this by practicing a restored ethic, a restored hope, a restored community, a restored peace, a restored truth, a restored love, and a restored reconciliation.[80]

Marginality

We must listen and learn from marginalized voices in this process—primarily Indigenous, Black, poor, immigrant, disabled, elderly, and female. Moreover, we must relinquish power and control and invite these groups to lead us as we seek the restoration of justice. Church and society have silenced and ignored these groups too often. We often find it challenging to listen to those on the margins. Today, many people are on the margins of society. They often feel socially excluded and invisible. People get pushed to the margins for various reasons: social class, race, skin color, religion, gender, disability, educational status, living choices, sexuality, and more. Who are the people that find themselves on the margins today? Many, including

---

80. Hill and Kim, *Healing Our Broken Humanity*, 95–97.

the elderly, the young, Muslims, people of color, Indigenous peoples, undocumented migrants, refugees, asylum seekers, many women, particular ethnic groups, impoverished families, caregivers, and those with disabilities—to name a few.

God doesn't only place the margins at the center of his love, concern, and mission. He begins movements there. And he speaks to society and culture and church from there. God's mission is from the margins. Jesus was a Galilean Jew. He didn't just care for the margins; he was from the margins himself. If the church's mission, ministry, and message reflect how God places the margins at the center of his love and concern, then the church must see the margins as not merely being incidental to the whole. We don't simply get a helpful perspective from the margins—God often speaks to us from there.

So, how do we listen to the margins? How do we hear even if we can't immediately see how the concerns of the margins affect us personally?

Here are seven practices that help us hear and respond to marginalized people.[81] We've listed them as steps, but, in truth, they are interwoven and often simultaneous. In *Healing Our Broken Humanity*, Grace Ji-Sun Kim and Graham unpack nine practices for revitalizing the church and renewing the world. We offer practical guidance on implementing them in small groups, teams, families, and congregations.

In what follows, we offer a shortened and summarized list of some key themes and chapters in *Healing Our Broken Humanity*. Quotations in this list come directly from that book. We encourage you to buy *Healing Our Broken Humanity* and engage in the small group practices we offer for each of these steps. The nine practices offered in the book are reimagine church, renew lament, repent together, relinquish power, restore justice, reactivate hospitality, reinforce agency, reconcile relationships, and recover life together.[82]

---

81. This list of seven steps was first published by Graham here: Hill, "Hearing and Responding."

82. Hill and Kim, *Healing Our Broken Humanity*.

1. Repent Together

The first step is to recognize and repent of our complicity in injustice, discrimination, and processes of marginalization. This isn't easy. We often don't see how we've contributed to the problem.

> We need to ask ourselves difficult questions. How have my attitudes and practices disadvantaged the elderly, Muslims, people of color, indigenous peoples, undocumented migrants or refugees, women, the poor, those with disabilities, and other groups? How have my choices, preferences, and attitudes silenced and marginalized these groups? How do my political decisions compound the problem? Then, how do I repent and embrace the mind of Christ?

> The Gospel of Luke describes Jesus's concern for those marginalized in society. Jesus identifies with the outcast. He prioritizes them. As said earlier, Jesus himself was from the margins. Jesus identifies with, welcomes, hears, and prioritizes the poor, the sinners, the women, the sick, the rejected, and the outcast. His concern for the margins is scandalous. It's in sharp contrast to his age's spirit and the nationalistic, uncompassionate religiosity of other religious leaders.

> Jesus calls us to repent of the things we've done—and the attitudes we've harbored—that serve to marginalize others. Jesus calls us to welcome, embrace, and listen to those marginalized by society for various reasons:
>
> - those marginalized because of their physical life (including the disabled, the elderly, and the sick).
>
> - those marginalized because of their race, ethnicity, or gender (including indigenous groups, people of color, and women).
>
> - those marginalized because of their religion, profession, or sexual orientation (including Muslims, sex workers, and same-sex-attracted persons).
>
> - those marginalized because of their political persuasions (including those who hold different political views than you).

Sweeping Pains

In this process of repentance, we join Jesus in compassion, welcome, and friendship. Jesus welcomes to table fellowship those who are usually shunned. Jesus was crucified because of the people he ate with. Our repentance leads us to the same table fellowship.[83]

2. Relinquish Power

The next step is equally difficult. We must relinquish power. For most of us, our power is found in our wealth, education, gender, profession, and race. Power can be destructive and divisive. But it can also be healing and nurturing when it is released and used for other's wellbeing and human flourishing. We relinquish power when we genuinely listen to those who've been marginalized. We relinquish control (and use what power we have for good) when we use all our energies to make sure we and others are hearing, respecting, profiling, honoring, and responding to the marginalized. We relinquish power when we seek to give power away and move the margins to a welcoming center—a multi-voiced, multi-peopled, multicultural, new creation, new humanity center.[84]

We relinquish power when we say "no" to opportunities so that other voices can be heard. We relinquish power when we say "yes" to justice and action so that other voices can be honored.

3. Restore Justice

In addition to relinquishing power, we should also seek to restore justice. This involves speaking and acting for justice. It means addressing injustice head-on. Sympathy must move to compassion, which must move to love, which must move to advocacy and action. Love without action is meaningless. Charity without justice is hollow. Solidarity without advocacy is only half the picture.

---

83. Hill and Kim, *Healing Our Broken Humanity*, 70–71.
84. Hill and Kim, *Healing Our Broken Humanity*, 78.

Restoring justice also involves listening to the concerns and perspectives of others, even when these seem to address issues that don't directly affect us. It consists in standing up for the rights and wellbeing of others—even if their wellbeing or prosperity or flourishing seems only indirectly related to ours, and even when their wellbeing comes at our expense.

This is about walking in other people's shoes. It's about addressing contemporary and historical injustices on behalf of others. We imitate the one who came into this world for our wellbeing—giving up his comfort, safety, power, and position. We follow the one who was wounded, bruised, rejected, and crucified for us. We imitate the one who restores justice in an unjust world.[85]

4. Reactivate Hospitality

As Christians, we should relish and respect diversity. Christianity is an extraordinary mosaic of cultures, peoples, ethnicities, traditions, theologies, personalities, and groups. The Spirit of Jesus Christ unifies us. The Spirit forges Christian unity. It's not our role to create harmony. It's our role to cultivate bonds of peace.

Where we feel we can't relish diversity, we should at least respect diversity. This means that we don't "lord it over" those who are different from us. We don't seek to colonize, patronize, domesticate, exclude, homogenize, attack, or silence them. We recognize Christ in the stranger and foreigner and offer welcome, hospitality, and embrace.

In pluralistic, multicultural, multireligious settings, respecting diversity also means respecting different religious or philosophical traditions and cultural backgrounds. We can hold firmly to our Christian convictions and beliefs while showing respect and honor to others.

---

85. Hill and Kim, *Healing Our Broken Humanity*, 95–96.

5. Reinforce Agency

Christians have essential roles to play in this regard. And, thankfully, we often do this in cooperation with other groups. Our part is to do the following:[86]

- Provide spaces for those at the margins to speak and be heard (supporting them as they articulate their concerns, interests, and perspectives). We must also reinforce agency. Agency is the capacity of a person or group to act independently, decisively, and freely in any given environment.
- Listen deeply and attentively to their perspectives and what God is saying to church, society, and culture through them.
- Resource them as they pursue and express agency.
- Stand with them as advocates and allies as they seek to name and understand their strengths, problems, and perspectives.
- Support those at the margins as they cultivate agency, voice, wellbeing, and human flourishing.
- Name the crucial relationship between the Christian gospel and the Galilean Jewish Jesus who was himself from the margins (and the triune God of Israel, who pursues his redemptive purposes from the margins of humanity and history).
- Find creative ways to ensure that the voices and perspectives of marginalized people are heard by political parties, politicians, and other elected and civic leaders.
- Join with those (through carefully selected Christian and non-Christian groups) who are seeking to ensure that these voices are heard, respected, and responded to during the current election.

6. Reconcile Relationships

We must also seek to renew partnerships and reconcile relationships.

[86]. Hill and Kim, *Healing Our Broken Humanity*, 133–35.

Sunburnt Country, Sweeping Pains

In *The Christian Imagination,* Willie James Jennings tells a story from his childhood. He tells a story about how white Christians were oblivious to African Americans' faith, dreams, and needs in their very street and neighborhood. Reconciled relationships [and true partnerships] are about genuinely *seeing* and *hearing* and *engaging with* the other. Such partnerships require us to work through power dynamics to become equal, mutual, and reciprocal partnerships. Marginalized people mustn't be recipients. They must be partners.[87]

7. Revitalize Church and Mission

Finally, the voices, perspectives, gifts, and graces of marginalized people can revitalize our churches and mission. We are also renewed as these seven practices lead us to form new theologies, habits, and relationships.

Jayakumar Christian reminds us that marginalized groups revitalize us as they do the following:[88]

1. Disrupt and disturb the status quo.
2. Challenge us to embrace holiness that's relational and inclusive.
3. Create ripples of transformation.
4. Lead us to form a whole-of-life, missional spirituality.

Marginalized groups enable us to become churches and Christians that reflect the values of God's kingdom and join with God in his mission in the world.

Intersectionality

Theologizing well about justice and marginality also requires us to develop a theology of intersectionality. Intersectionality has a bad name in some quarters of church and society. Many conservatives

---

[87]. Hill and Kim, *Healing Our Broken Humanity,* 141; Jennings, *Christian Imagination,* 2–3.
[88]. Hill, "4 Qualities of Missional Movements."

have weaponized the concept of intersectionality. On the other hand, many progressives have diluted or distorted it. The definition, scope, and value of intersectionality are contested, just as definitions of race and gender are contested. One only needs to look at the debate surrounding Sally Haslanger's book *Resisting Reality* or Angela Y. Davis's book *Women, Race and Class* to see the feeling, ideology, rhetoric, and analysis surrounding these debates.[89]

Intersectionality was first conceived in 1989 by Black feminist scholar Kimberlé Williams Crenshaw. Intersectionality describes how various aspects of a person's social, racial, gendered, and political identity intersect, overlap, and combine to determine their experience of discrimination and privilege. In "Mapping the Margins: Intersectionality, Identity Politics, and Violence Against Women of Color," Crenshaw shows how three different forms of intersectionality affect violence against women, especially women of color.[90] The three forms outlined are *structural intersectionality* (classism, sexism, and racism combining and overlapping in systems of oppression); *political intersectionality* (political institutions ignoring the violence against women of color, even while they seek to address sexism and racism); and *representational intersectionality* (the sexist and racist representation of women of color in imagery, media, film, and so on). Naturally, all three forms of intersectionality affect Asian Australian women and all women of color in Australia.

As Gale A. Yee writes, it is time for us to think intersectionally. Gender, race, class, and other aspects of our social and political identities combine and overlap in multiple, complex, and often unacknowledged ways to influence and shape our church life, mission, biblical interpretations, theology, and treatment of minoritized groups among us. Yee says:

> Intersectional analyses make the fundamental point that we who study and interpret the biblical text have many important facets to our identities that are impacted differently by multiple interacting systems of

89. Haslanger, *Resisting Reality*; Davis, *Women, Race and Class*. See, for instance: Haslanger, "Race, Intersectionality, and Method"; Jones, "Intersectionality"; Jihye Chun et al., "Social Movement Strategy."
90. Crenshaw, "Mapping the Margins."

oppression and privilege. As a method of interpretation, intersectionality presumes that our own unique social locations, our own distinctive fusions of gender, race, class, et cetera, influence our readings of texts and our interpretations of them. It encourages us to think beyond the familiar boundaries of biblical studies to expose the diverse power relations of inequality in the text and uncover subjugated voices that were previously invisible or unheard.[91]

Thinking and theologizing intersectionally is vital for all aspects of church life and ministry. We contend that there is no way to deal with the complex nature of injustice and marginalization without theologizing and thinking in terms of intersectionality. Gale A. Yee and Patricia Hill Collins show us why the church cannot ignore intersectionality when addressing injustices and especially the violence and discrimination experienced by women of color. Here we quote the assumptions undergirding this conviction:

1. Race, class, gender, sexuality, age, ability, nation, ethnicity, and similar categories of analysis are best understood in relational terms rather than in isolation from one another.
2. These mutually constructing categories underlie and shape intersecting systems of power; the power relations of racism and sexism, for example, are interrelated.
3. Intersecting systems of power, such as racism and sexism, catalyze social formations of complex social inequalities. These social formations are organized by means of unequal material realities and the distinctive social experiences for people who live within them.
4. Because social formations of complex social inequalities are historically contingent and cross-culturally specific, unequal material realities and social experiences vary across time and space.
5. Individuals and groups who are placed differently within intersecting systems of power have diverse points of view on their own and others' experiences with complex social inequalities,

---

91. Yee, "Thinking Intersectionally," 7.

typically advancing projects that reflect their social locations within power relations.

The complex social inequalities fostered by intersecting systems of power are fundamentally unjust, shaping projects and/or political engagements that uphold or contest the status quo.[92]

One of the most valuable guides to intersectional theology is Grace Ji-Sun Kim and Susan M. Shaw's book *Intersectional Theology: An Introductory Guide*. Kim and Shaw show us how to develop intersectional theology and practice. They challenge us "to imagine an intersectional church, a practice of welcome and inclusion rooted in an ecclesiology that embraces difference and centers social justice."[93] We need a theology of justice, marginality, and intersectionality.

OFFERING A REDEMPTIVE ALTERNATIVE TO THE CULTURE WARS

Western and Asian societies politicize culture, race, sexuality, religion, and gender. The church often participates in this politicization. James Davison Hunter popularized the notion of "culture wars" in his groundbreaking book *Culture Wars: The Struggle to Define America*.[94] In that book, Hunter argued that the culture wars are about the orthodox versus the progressive. This contest is sometimes expressed with religious associations, but not always. While progressives and conservatives often engage in the culture wars through debates about morality, the heart of the issue is usually identity. In that ideologically and politically charged environment, it's typical for conservatives and progressives to fail to hear

---

92. Yee, "Thinking Intersectionally," 11–12. Yee is summarizing Collins, "Intersectionality's Definitional Dilemmas," 14.

93. Kim and Shaw, *Intersectional Theology*. From the back cover.

94. Hunter, *Culture Wars*. For sample works addressing cultural, racial, and gendered politics in contemporary Asia, see Zheng, *Cultural Politics*; Kim, "Understanding 'Koreanness.'"

each other. Radical conservatives caricature and demonize progressive positions and claim to be victims. Zealous progressives engage in witch hunts, cancel culture, and intimidation. Culture, race, and gender get swept up in the politics of the culture wars, and divisions and antagonism become widespread and entrenched. Christians need to confront and transcend cultural and gender politics and the animosities of the culture wars if we want to witness to Christ, his gospel and kingdom, and the new humanity he creates.

Confronting cultural and gender politics isn't simple. Determining the right stance is complex. But if Bible-believing Christians begin with antagonism and attacking society and culture, we will make no gains. Christians need to welcome culture as a conversation partner and join God's Spirit in the world.[95] Christians often fear culture and cultural change. We treat culture as the enemy and act out of fear and defensiveness. Conversely, Christianity is often associated with a wide range of negative ideas and themes. The church too often adopts the ideologies of the world, which express themselves as antagonism, conflict, indifference, and fear. There are many examples. We may promote partisan politics and fear cultural change. We may reject those who do not hold to a rigid form of Calvinism or fundamentalism. We may embrace nationalism and sanction militarism. We may encourage racial and gender discrimination. Sometimes we act as moral police while avoiding real scrutiny. We might equate white middle-class values and lifestyles with the gospel. We're tempted to avoid scholarship and independent thought. We may conflate capitalism with the good Christian life. We might fear science and literature and higher criticism. We may endorse immoral politicians and form questionable alliances for short-term social or political gain. The list is long.

But being conformed to Christ is about rejecting narrow, fear-based, exclusive, partisan, politicized, and combative faith. Conformity means embracing a generous, inclusive, humble, and love-based commitment to people and the gospel. A conformed church is committed to Christ, evangelism, gospel-faithfulness, and Scripture. Such a church also pursues social justice, cultural

---

95. Hill, *Salt, Light, and a City*, 332–33.

renewal, racial and gender justice, ministering in the power of the Spirit, holistic ministry, political action, and creation care, peacemaking, and reconciliation. This faith is generous and embracing. This posture is faithful to the gospel and conforms to the image of the Son. Conformity to the image of the Son always expresses itself as humility, love, maturity, peace, justice, and prophetic truthtelling—as a social ethic formed in the image of Christ.

Let's stop treating the culture as our enemy. Let's also stop imitating and uncritically adopting the values and perspectives of culture and society. Culture is our counterpoint, mirror, conversation partner, protagonist, foil, enricher, and more. We must be socially and culturally engaged since we are always culturally located. Being culturally engaged and located does not mean being socially and culturally reduced. Instead, we explore where society, culture, and theology have enriched, shaped, and shackled each other. Sometimes all these things are happening at once.

The church needs to enter a creative conversation with a wide range of disciplines. This conversation is two-way. These disciplines include ethics, politics, philosophy, cultural studies, sociology, social theories, postcolonialism, gender and racial studies, cultural intelligence, aesthetics, creative arts, ecology, health, education, business and leadership studies, history, and more. This means seeing Scripture as our highest authority and exploring how God is speaking to us and his world through culture and a wide range of disciplines, and seeing where God is present and moving in the world. This posture enables us to respond creatively, courageously, and redemptively to the painful experiences of Asian Australian women in mission and ministry. We can address injustices and systemic oppressions while firmly holding the gospel and truth of our Lord Jesus Christ.

We pray that the church would reflect God's passion for justice, mercy, self-relinquishment, and humble service. We hope that God's people would be radical and activistic, addressing the systems of power and privilege that intersect to marginalize, silence, and oppress (including sexism, racism, classism, exceptionalism, ableism, ageism, nationalism, and nativism). We call for God's people to rise above the antagonisms and divisions of the culture wars. We desire that the church see God's hand and hear God's voice from and in the margins of society and the church. We yearn for God's people to be a healing, prophetic, shalomic, and redemptive presence in a divided, unjust, and broken world.

3

Far Horizons

Women are the Heartbeat of Living Faith

HONORING WOMEN'S GIFTS AND CONTRIBUTIONS

Women are, and always have been, the heartbeat of living faith.[1] Diana Butler Bass used that phrase in a recent interview, and we love it. Women are at the center of Christian faith, discipleship, worship, ministry, theology, community, and mission.

Stephen Bevans recently wrote:

> We are now living in a "world church" where the vast majority of Christians are [from the Majority World]. David Barrett's statistical studies have confirmed this shift, and Philip Jenkins has predicted that by 2025 fully two-thirds of Christians will live in Africa, Latin America, and Asia . . . Scholars are fairly unanimous in acknowledging the accuracy of the facts. The "average

---

1. Graham first published these thoughts here: Hill, "Women Are the Heartbeat." He later offered them in a modified form: Hill, *Holding Up Half the Sky*, 12–14.

Christian" today is female, black, and lives in a Brazilian *favela* or an African village.²

Globally, Christian women are more spiritually active than men and more persecuted.

Recently asked what it would mean for Christian women if a woman became President, Diana Butler Bass responded this way:

> I hope that we will finally get beyond the idea of "Christian women leaders" being some special subset of Christian community. Women are the majority of Christians around the world—*we are the heartbeat of living faith.* The media spends too much time covering male leaders—and then a small subset of authoritarian conservative men—as if they are the voice of the church. They are not. Women are. All the women. The women who preach, the women who write theology, the women who pray, the women who serve, those who hold the hand of the dying. Those who care for children, those who feed the hungry, those who embrace the poor and visit prisoners. Those who weep and mourn for the pain they've suffered. Those who find that God's love is more beautiful and trustworthy than those who abused them. That's the church—a church that knows no facile forgiveness or partisan spin. But the church that understands grace, peacemaking, and mercy. And that church is rarely heard in public because it is too busy living its faith.³

Reta Halteman helped us see that nothing shaped the early church's theology, community, and mission more than the people at its heart.⁴ These people were women, the poor, the sick, the outcast, the powerless, and the marginalized. These groups formed the nucleus of the ancient church. They understood themselves as following the example and mission of Christ.

Men had a vital role to play, of course. Men have an essential part in the church today. Women and men and children—of all ethnicities and languages and income and social classes—must

2. Bevans et al., "Missiology after Bosch," 69.
3. Crumm, "Diana Butler Bass." Emphases added.
4. Finger, *Widows and Meals*.

come together as a new family and new humanity in Christ. But for thousands of years, men have had all the power, recognition, opportunities, and voice. We've neglected the people who are the heartbeat of living faith.

Women, the poor, the sick, the outcast, the powerless, and the marginalized weren't just a part of the early church community. They didn't just heavily influence the early church community. They were at the heart of the community. Women, the poor, and the socially marginalized shaped the theology, fellowship, service, discipleship, and mission of the early church. These groups shaped these things in immense and invaluable ways.

Jesus reinvents the family. He creates an intentional community. The early church was a community of open homes, economic sharing, communal meals, and spiritual family. Within this extended family, people met each other's economic and social needs. These churches abolished the acquisition of wealth and honor by patronage. They met daily in homes and around meals. They prized loyalty, love, faith, welcome, hospitality, hope, diversity, equality, truth-telling, and grace.

Jesus chose women to be at the heart of this community. Their love, hospitality, and passion shaped the early church. The same is true today, all over the globe. Women are the heartbeat of living faith. They are the voice, hands, and heart of the church. Jesus reimagines family and household and male/female relations. This has profound implications for the church. It has massive consequences for our theologies, gender relations, communal sharing, and mission in the world. It has allowed women all over the church to rise, use their gifts, and show leadership.

Phoebe, for instance, was a highly regarded woman in the church of Cenchreae; a deacon, and a respected patron. The hospitable women of Acts 2, 4, and 6 are sometimes hidden in the text. But they're the backbone of the church and its mission. These women showed that faith isn't merely a private or religious affair. These women's actions reveal the power of the gospel to shape the social, political, sexual, economic, ethical, and other aspects of our lives.

Women were crucial to shaping the early church and turning it into a family on mission. Women continue to do the same today.

Sunburnt Country, Sweeping Pains

It shouldn't surprise us that women are the heartbeat of living faith. As Dorothy Sayers once observed, women have met a Man like no other. And they choose to follow him and shape a church that reflects his welcome, diversity, equality, and kinship. Sayers writes:

> Perhaps it is no wonder that the women were first at the Cradle and last at the Cross. They had never known a man like this Man—there never has been such another. A prophet and teacher who never nagged at them, never flattered or coaxed or patronized; who never made arch jokes about them, never treated them either as "The women, God help us!" or "The ladies, God bless them!"; who rebuked without querulousness and praised without condescension; who took their questions and arguments seriously; who never mapped out their sphere for them, never urged them to be feminine or jeered at them for being female; who had no axe to grind and no uneasy male dignity to defend; who took them as he found them and was completely unself-conscious. There is no act, no sermon, no parable in the whole Gospel that borrows its pungency from female perversity; nobody could possibly guess from the words and deeds of Jesus that there was anything "funny" about woman's nature.[5]

Jesus honored and welcomed women. He invited them to join him in forming a new spiritual family. Jesus asked them to carry his message and vision, embodying his love and welcome and peacemaking. He invited them to join fully with him in his mission. So, in the ancient and modern church, locally and globally, women are the heartbeat of living faith.

In this chapter, we explore the talents, contributions, and perspectives of the Asian Australian women who participated in our research. These women are a gift and grace to the Australian church and beyond.

---

5. Sayers, *Are Women Human?*, 90. For a South Asian perspective on Jesus's honoring of marginalized women, see Sadiq, "Jesus' Encounter."

UNIQUE ROLES AND ATTITUDES

We asked these women their views on Asian Australian women's unique contributions to mission, ministry, service, evangelism, and social justice. Here is a summary of the things these women said in response to this question.

Asian Australian women are often able to connect with vulnerable women and other ethnic groups in society. These women often empathize with international students, refugees, and outsiders. These women can open doors and inhabit multiple cultural spaces. The women we interviewed said things like this: "Asian women can inhabit spaces of color and learn what the needs are, which is special, while also being more accepted in white spaces (problematic, because it's due to the 'model minority stereotype' but can still be helpful to people of color). Asian women can help open the door to their other Brown and Black siblings."[6] "I believe Asian background women can enrich a multicultural ministry or embody the equality of genders. The particular strength is in the ability to minister among the vulnerable and marginalized."[7] One woman wrote of the ability of Asian peoples to serve with Indigenous peoples. "The colonizing treatment of Indigenous people has made barriers to white mission and service, but the barriers are not as significant for Asians."[8]

Asian Australian women are often "versatile when it comes to serving on the mission field. They can do anything (technology, language abilities, well-educated, work experiences, able to understand the Asian mentality, and cultural competencies, etc.)."[9] These women can more easily connect in Asian mission fields and ministry contexts. They can also bridge cultures since many of these women have been doing this their whole lives. "For those of us who have grown up in two cultures, adding a third or fourth culture in missions is often an easier transition. We have always lived cross-culturally between our Australian and Asian backgrounds and

---

6. Research participant twenty-five.
7. Research participant twenty-seven.
8. Research participant three.
9. Research participant eight.

often understand the subtleties of indirect communication. We can be a bridge between the Western and local cultures."[10] The marginality these Asian Australian women have experienced their whole lives can also be used for the sake of others. These women bring "a unique background as bicultural and bilingual and more cultural awareness and more openness to the other. These women have a more open way of engaging and bringing the voices of the global south and the east. The margin is the gift."[11]

In many Asian Christian contexts, evangelism and word-based ministries are emphasized over welfare, service, and social justice ministries. This can be a barrier to Asian Australian women engaging in activism, justice, and compassion ministries. But it can also motivate them to push through these barriers and integrate word and action, evangelism and justice, compassion and mercy, gospel proclamation and political advocacy, and so on. A few women noted that the emphasis varies depending on the Asian cultural background and theological tradition. Some Asian cultures and theological traditions are more word-based and gospel-centered, focusing on proclamation and charity rather than justice and advocacy. Like many Filipino churches, others emphasize justice, peacemaking, welfare, and social transformation. Almost all the women discussed their wrestles with these issues. These women talked about their efforts to serve in mission and ministry and make a difference in church and society. "Most of the Asian Australian women I know on the mission field are passionate, thoughtful, energetic . . . They're out to protect the vulnerable, shout from soapboxes, and spread all of Jesus's good news and love to anyone who will listen. They champion those who can't champion themselves, and they work super hard."[12]

We proceed to address two critical questions. First, how is the church's witness enhanced by encouraging more Asian Australian women into ministry and mission? Second, how can Australian

---

10. Research participant fifteen.
11. Research participant eleven.
12. Research participant twenty-one.

Christians address racism, sexism, and inequality, while releasing more Asian Australian women to ministry and mission?

Answering these questions wasn't always easy for these women, as they recounted difficult experiences. One woman wrote, "There are racism and discrimination within Asian contexts. I feel discriminated against as the Asian wife of a white male. There is sometimes ethnic tension between the various Chinese groups. There is still a male, hierarchical powerbase that you need to submit to in Asian churches, so to even get on to the mission field, you need to be in favor with those people."[13] Another said:

> Often churches are either entirely Asian or mostly white, and so being an Asian woman on the leadership team can make ministry difficult. They have trouble relating to me. Too many groups stick to their own culture. I can feel they don't know how to relate to me as an Asian woman. I often feel like an outsider and like I am on my own. Some churches seem afraid of migrants, and the impact migrants will have on their identity and community. Do we exist to be just a social club for Christians, or what is our real mission? If our focus is on keeping our white identity, then the future is diminishing.[14]

Yet, these women have hope for change and that their gifts and contributions will make a difference in church and society. "I hope that working together in ministry brings people together from across cultural and ethnic backgrounds. We must be willing to open up and welcome people to participate and focus on building deeper relations, not just welcoming people on a surface level, but truly sharing relationship, life, power, and leadership."[15]

ENHANCING THE CHURCH'S WITNESS

White progressive Christianity has a problem. White progressives often feel proud of their progressivism and unable to see

13. Research participant thirty.
14. Research participant eighteen.
15. Research participant ten.

their sexism, racism, and complicity in systems and structures of discrimination. In their efforts to address injustices and appear enlightened, white progressives too often speak "for" other groups and assume they know what marginalized groups want to say and contribute.

The racism within white feminism is an example of this. Aboriginal theologian Anne Pattel-Gray writes:

> Hypocrisy is found in the feminist movement to the point that this privileged group defines and determines the particular feminist interests as representing the common interest of all women. Somehow these feminists spend a great deal of time and energy proving that their views reflect universal values, that encompass all women within Australia. If this is so, then feminists need to consider how much they distort reality in order to maintain their interests. It is quite obvious that there is a need for Australian feminists to address and confront their own racism and classism, and the status that they enjoy because they are white and how, because of their color, privilege is obtained and maintained within society...
>
> Aboriginal women's freedom is limited by the racism of Australian feminism. Our origins are different and our histories are incomparable. Our experiences of Australian church feminism, in the past and in the present, confirm pervasive racism. We do not need women who are trapped by their own complicity, and continue to benefit from our suffering and exclusion. In short, we do not need to be liberated by our oppressors. Rather, Aboriginal women of Australia welcome women who are willing to learn, and learn—to open their hearts. Then, perhaps, we will walk forward as *tiddas* (sisters).[16]

Similarly, it would be a mistake for those of us who are not Asian Australian women to assume we know how the church's witness is enhanced by releasing more Asian Australian women to local church work or local and overseas missions. It is crucial, therefore, that we listen to these women.

---

16. Pattel-Gray, *Great White Flood*, 185–86.

The women told us that there are numerous ways in which the participation and leadership of Asian Australian women enhance the church's ministry and local and overseas missions. These women have hybrid identities and sensibilities. Being part of a collectivist and an individualist culture helps them to see many cultures at work. They can be flexible to work and serve in various structures and systems. They adapt as needed. This courage helps these women adapt to new cultures and expectations. They can adjust to new ways of thinking and doing things. They can understand individualistic and collectivistic cultures.

Asian Australian women are great facilitators, peacemakers, ambassadors, and women who understand different cultural values and contexts. First-generation women know the experience of learning a language, being marginalized, and being an immigrant, and these understandings help them connect with those in a similar situation. Increased diversity opens the door for other minorities. Equality and diversity show Christian leadership's willingness to value the voices of those who are on the margins and reach out and embrace those of different and varied cultures.

These women are gifted and called by God to serve in mission and ministry. The church should be the kingdom of God made visible. If it consists only of white people or only men, how can the gospel be good news for the whole world? In Genesis, God called humans to multiply and fill the earth. We understand that this mission required both the man and the woman. Jesus called us to fill the earth and multiply disciples. That requires both men and women. Releasing more women and, in the case of this study, more Asian Australian women, enables the church to reach more people with the love and gospel of Jesus Christ.

The inclusion and amplification of the gifts and leadership abilities of these Asian Australian women requires the church to change. One cultural, linguistic, and gender group's dominance is not healthy for the church or its mission and ministry. These women bring variety and diverse perspectives so that those of one cultural background are not the only ones to lead the church. Churches need to change to reflect the kingdom of God. This change includes releasing Asian women and showing a willingness to include other cultures. This inclusion is an example of how Christians should treat others of different backgrounds.

One woman put it powerfully. "If humans are the image of God and if the church is God's kingdom made visible, then every person ought to be represented. By releasing Asian women to church ministry, we demonstrate that we believe what Paul wrote in Galatians 3:28. We're also demonstrating that we trust the Holy Spirit to pour out gifts as he sees fit, regardless of our preconceived notions and prejudices."[17] Over half the global church are women. How can we not fully empower and release more than half the church to the calling of God on their lives to serve and witness to Christ?

ADDRESSING RACISM, SEXISM, AND INEQUALITY

It would be a mistake for those of us who are not Asian Australian women to assume we know how to bring change and deal with the inequalities, racism, or sexism we have discussed. It would also be an error to think we know what support Asian Australian women need to enter fully into ministry and mission. So, we asked these women this question: "How do we deal with racism, sexism, and inequality while releasing more Asian Australian women to ministry and mission?" Here is a summary of the suggestions made by these Asian Australian women.

1. Churches and mission agencies need to develop equality and diversity policies and abide by them. Leaders should ensure that members are well informed about these policies and matters. There should be reporting systems in place in case racism, discrimination, or sexism arise. We need accountability, discipline, and culture shift.
2. Pastors and mission leaders need to encourage equality and diversity in every possible way. If our boards and leadership teams aren't diverse, how can we say we are committed to hospitality, welcome, and diversity?

---

17. Research participant twenty-three.

3. Christian organizations should confront those with sexist and racist views and help them see the hurt and pain caused by their behaviors. Silence is complicity. The church is too often silent in the presence of sexism and racism. It's time to confront injustice and discrimination and to help people with these views see the pain and trauma caused by their microaggressions, positions, and actions. Eugene Cho writes:

> We have to ask how we are as revolutionary followers of Jesus—who debunked the systemic structures during his life—are working, living, ministering, writing, speaking, and creating to work towards that end? Power, voice, and influence are not easily pursued [and obtained]. It must be distributed and shared from those who have that very power, voice, and influence. And because it is so counter-cultural, we must be that much more intentional. As a male, I am embarrassed at times at how we [men] directly, indirectly, or systemically oppress our sisters.[18]

4. Organizations should pay women equally and appropriately. Women are paid poorly and inappropriately in too many Christian organizations. Women get relegated to part-time or low-paying positions and overlooked for promotions. This must change.
5. Treat women with equal respect and dignity afforded to their husbands. Asian Australian women recounted painful experiences of being silenced, overlooked, or ignored, even when they had more expertise and experience than their spouses.
6. Churches, mission agencies, and other Christian organizations should host constructive and open conversations about racism, sexism, inequalities, and discrimination. These discussions must lead to action. Racism, sexism, and inequality are within our churches and Christian organizations and not just out in society. It is essential to acknowledge, address, talk about this, and call it out. We often use polarizing and oppositional language within the church, which entrenches an "us versus them" language. We need to stop this.

---

18. Cho, "My Quasi-Conversation."

7. Have women on leadership teams who model leadership and who other women can go to when they need to discuss issues.
8. It is time to engage in the work of individual and collective decolonizing. This work involves creating processes that encourage more diverse voices at all levels of leadership. Start telling the truth about racism and sexism. Do some "white fragility" workshops. Stop being afraid to confront and tell the truth about the issues.
9. We need cultural intelligence training for churches and all leadership levels. The church and its leaders need more cultural competency (and to live out this value, rather than just talking about it). There seems more talk about cultural competency in Christian circles than the practice of it. The challenge is that when people of minority ethnic backgrounds come to Christian leaders for help, these leaders do not understand these people's cultural and relational experiences. The real challenge is loving and serving minority groups and showing cultural competence, sensitivity, and respect. Christian organizations and churches must feature cultural awareness in every way. Feature it in preaching, teaching, and leadership selection. Allow space during worship services to feature stories of people from diverse and minority cultural and ethnic backgrounds.
10. Acknowledging First Peoples and the pain of colonization. All churches need to work toward justice and reconciliation. This work is essential not just for white churches and Christians but for our Asian churches too. We all need to stand in solidarity with those who are marginalized.
11. Christians need theological training on the implications of having a theology of the Trinity, Pentecost, and the new humanity in Jesus Christ. These can inform what diversity and equality look like, how we pursue and practice them, and how they reflect God.
12. Reserve seats on councils and boards for people of marginalized identities.
13. Require that most members and the leader for initiatives aimed at marginalized communities be people of the same identity as those communities.

14. Teach children about inequalities and social justice when they are young.
15. Christian leaders need a change of heart that comes through repenting of racism and sexism. Leadership determines what churches value and how they look. If leaders do not change their attitudes and perspectives, then racism and sexism will continue. There are many programs that we can initiate and implement. But the most important thing is a change of heart. In *Holding Up Half the Sky*, we hear that "Jesus drives us from control to service, from competition to love, from a scarcity mindset to a generous spirit, from pride to humility, from ambition to self-denial, from drivenness to servanthood, from ego strength to interdependent vigor, and from identification with the powerful to servantship."[19]
16. Promote, mentor, and encourage Asian Australian Christian women. Train, equip, and release women. Recognize that appraisal, mentoring, and training may work differently in different cultures. Give Asian women opportunities in mission and ministry. Trust them. Confess our underlying assumptions and hidden presumptions that arise out of our insecurities and hunger for power. Power is given to us to serve, not for control or exercising our own biases. Offer more mentoring and leadership opportunities for women. Invite more Asian Australian women to "take the stage," so to speak, and share their experiences, wisdom, and insights.
17. Take the time to listen to Asian women's stories. But this alone is not sufficient. The church needs to repent of microaggressions, discrimination, and ignorance (which can be a sin of omission). The church needs to apologize to Asian women and all women. The church needs to empathize and demonstrate empathy intentionally. The church can give credit where credit is due, especially when women develop the ideas or do the work. Christians can find creative ways to include women in places of influence to make meaningful contributions. We

---

19. Hill, *Holding Up Half the Sky*, 89.

also need to include many minority voices, not just one person (which groups often do in a tokenistic way).
18. The church needs to be honest about who makes up the body of Christ and that for too long, it has catered to a very Western androcentric perspective. Church history, missiology, and theology focus on white Western philosophies, stories, missiologies, and theologies.
19. Dismantle systems of injustice and discrimination that hold women and minorities back from full and meaningful contribution and leadership.
20. Church and mission agency staff and leadership must be diverse, including women, minority groups, and Indigenous peoples.
21. Australian churches need to learn to see Asian people, their contributions, and their needs. As a community, they've been ignored. The church also needs to learn to see Jesus and other biblical figures for what they are (not white Europeans) and not what we imagine them to be.
22. Egalitarians must continue to fight for a better understanding of Scripture and its teachings on gender. Egalitarians also need to live out what they say they believe and value.
23. Prioritize gifting over gender in ministry.

> If a woman has a gift of leadership, let her lead. If a woman has a gift of teaching, let her teach. If a woman has a gift of prophecy, let her prophesy. These gifts, given by the Spirit to both women and men, should be fanned into flame and encouraged. The criteria for these gifts isn't gender but rather character and a commitment to the gospel. And there must be godly order and respect for local church leadership and a striving to edify, exhort, console, instruct, and commit to credible public witness. Such criteria apply equally to women and men and their use of their gifts.[20]

24. Many Asian Australian women come from church backgrounds that prevent or limit their contributions, so they are

---

20. Hill, *Holding Up Half the Sky*, 74.

often not encouraged. Help women find ministry and mission pathways beyond church settings that hold them back.

25. Educate Asian women about their rights and equality and encourage them to serve in mission and ministry. Because of many Asian cultures' views, Asian women may tend to step back and let other people help and lead.
26. Promote Asian women into theological education positions. It is almost impossible for Asian Australian women to get lecturing roles in theological institutions. Many Asian women do advanced theological and research degrees but can't find teaching roles and give up. Given the history of employing mainly white men, our theological seminaries and colleges need to prioritize hiring these Asian women.
27. Create networks for Asian women in mission and ministry. These networks help them find role models, mentors, build platforms, and support each other. Networks also amplify their voices and encourage younger emerging Asian women leaders in the future.
28. Keep telling stories about Asian Australian women who have gone into local ministry and overseas missions. The stories of others inspire us. Talking about the experiences of these women also fosters greater understanding and acceptance.
29. Offer more outreach and mission-focused tasks led by women with an Asian ethnic background. Encourage them to share what is in their hearts about ways to meet the needs of communities. Equip them with the skills they need to lead teams that can work to meet those needs.
30. Allocate missions funds dedicated to partnering with Asian Australian women in local and overseas missions. Provide the financial and other resources they need. Offer the pastoral care and supervision they need while fulfilling their service and mission.
31. Let Asian women take charge, lead, and take the initiative.
32. Christian conferences can intentionally target and encourage Asian women to go into mission and ministry.
33. Give scholarships to Asian Australian women to go to seminary. Mentoring, scholarships, paid internships, and more

diverse seminaries are key. Support academic and career progression.

34. Do not do overseas missions unless you have multiple people from that country or ethnicity on the planning committee.
35. Offer Asian women access to strengths-based tests and training. Be intentional. Identify the strengths and gifts of Asian Australian women and empower them to minister accordingly.
36. Learn to see Asian people beyond the stereotypes and the otherness. See their unique individual personalities, gifts, and callings. See how they image God and the kingdom of heaven. Do not make Asian peoples fight to be seen. Meet them halfway. Treat Asian women with dignity and respect and as equals.

We finish this discussion with quotations from three interview subjects, slightly modified or paraphrased for grammatical purposes. These are the concluding remarks of three women to our interviews and synopsize what many of these women said to us in the interview's final stages.

Churches and mission agencies are becoming more ethnically and culturally diverse. One woman writes:

> The temptation for those from the majority European-ethnic cultures of Australia, North America, and European contexts is to treat Asian ethnic peoples like a threat or to be indifferent to them and their contributions. Or to treat them like victims who need our help. None of these responses are healthy. Asian Australian women are not a threat and are certainly not victims and can make a significant difference to church and mission. Christian churches and mission agencies and their leaders need to treat Asians as friends and equals. A study like this one can be dangerous and even potentially misleading. There are some disadvantages faced by Asian Australian women in mission and ministry, but these women learn to navigate life and ministry as both Asian and female. These women are strong, insightful, and determined to make a difference. These women do not spend their lives feeling unfairly treated or victimized. What migrants and women in ministry and mission need most is equal

friendship—feeling respected, equal, and friends. Helping can hurt when we do not act as equals. We should not see Asian women as victims who need help or protection (or an opportunity for inclusion). Asian women need opportunities because of their gifts, skills, perseverance, and hard work. We must treat them as equals. What is most important is welcome, respect, dignity, and equality.[21]

Another woman says, "A study like this should lead churches and mission agencies to further self-examination. Are we truly interested in learning from other cultures' theology and faith (listening and learning for the theology from within other cultures and perspectives)? Are we open to seeing the God we worship from the margins (who can be very different from the God we worship from the privileged position)?"[22]

Finally, a third woman finished her interview with these challenging words. "Working together in mission and ministry can bring people together from across cultural, gender, and ethnic backgrounds. These Asian Australian women invite the church to open and welcome people into full participation. They challenge us to build deeper and more equal relationships, not just to welcome people on a surface level, but truly sharing relationship, life, power, and leadership."[23]

This cooperation for a more just, hospitable world requires a more diverse, welcoming church and Christians working with other religious, secular, and activist groups for societal change. Sun Ai Lee-Park and Sang Jung Park offer crucial challenges for the Australian church's mission in a diverse, pluralistic society. Christians in the Asia-Pacific, including Australia, are in a missionary situation.

> We are surrounded by people of other living faiths. For many of us, it is a serious question whether we can build a just society as Christians alone. We have been

21. Research participant eighteen.
22. Research participant nineteen.
23. Research participant twenty.

convinced that we must find ways to cooperate and dialogue with people of other faiths for our common task in our respective societies. This means in one sense that our efforts for building genuine community must always have some spillover effect. We need to ask what the visible reality of that effect would be. Let us remember that in the communities of people of other faiths there are also persons seriously committed to building authentic human community as they understand it. And our attempts should not be mutually exclusive. After all, *the women of Asia hold more than half of the sky and nurture more than half of the earth.*[24]

THE VITALITY OF ASIAN WOMEN'S THEOLOGY AND PRACTICES, AND THE DANGER OF AUSTRALIAN IMAGES OF MASCULINITY

Many Asian Australian women offer their voices, theologies, and practices from the margins of church and society and the fringe of theological discourse. These women hail from diverse ethnicities, cultures, linguistic backgrounds, theological traditions, and social locations. Their contributions to Christian theology, mission vitality, and ministry practices are profound, unsettling, beautiful, and provocative.[25] These are theologies and practices that challenge prevailing wisdom, upend accepted norms, and point to radical and activistic church life, witness, and beliefs. Striving against the shackles of discrimination and speaking and writing regardless of oppression and marginalization, these Asian Australian women offer the Australian church liberating and prophetic messages and examples. Like their Asian American sisters, these Asian Australian women support and invest in church and society through their blood, sweat, prayers, labor, and tears. As Sucheta Mazumdar says

---

24. Lee-Park and Park, "Woman and Man in Community," 155. Emphases added.

25. For striking examples of the theology of Asian and Asian diaspora women, see Orevillo-Montenegro, *Jesus of Asian Women*; Kyung, *Struggle to Be*.

of Asian women of the diaspora, "They are pioneer women. Instead of investing money, they are investing suffering."[26]

In *The Strength of Her Witness*, Elizabeth A. Johnson gathers female theological contributions from the global voices of women (from the United States, Nigeria, Canada, Australia, South Korea, the Philippines, Kenya, Ghana, Vanuatu, Brazil, Mexico, Germany, Aboriginal peoples, Hong Kong, and India). Johnson quotes Elisabeth Schüssler Fiorenza, who writes:

> According to all four gospels, Mary Magdalene is the primary witness for the fundamental data of the early Christian faith: she witnessed the life and death of Jesus, his burial and resurrection. She was sent to the disciples to proclaim the Easter kerygma. Therefore, Bernard of Clairvaux correctly calls her "apostle to the apostles." Christian faith is based upon the witness and proclamation of women. As Mary Magdalene was sent to the disciples to proclaim the basic events of Christian faith, so women today may rediscover by contemplating her image the important function and role which they have for the Christian faith and community.[27]

There is too much focus on masculinity in the global church. But Christ isn't a white man nor the epitome of "masculinity" or "biblical manhood." Graham recently wrote an article for CBE International challenging this focus on masculinity and femininity and calling the church back to a focus on discipleship.[28]

> The masculinity movement is now an entire industry with books, seminars, and speakers. The movement has grown up around notions of "biblical manhood," but in reality, it reinforces worldly ideas of masculinity and femininity. Today, a whole generation of boys and men

---

26. Mazumdar, "Beyond Bound Feet," 27.

27. Johnson, *Strength of Her Witness*, 1. From Schüssler Fiorenza, *Discipleship of Equals*, 77. For a brilliant book on Asian women's theology, see Park and Fabella, *We Dare to Dream*.

28. Hill, "Let's Stop Talking." First rights notice: "This article first appeared in CBE International's blog, *Mutuality*, on 01/08/2020 (www.cbeinternational.org)."

are looking for guidance on how to live as men, and the Christian masculinity industry feeds on their feelings of longing and insecurity. Sadly, the solutions it offers cause further damage. Additionally, a lot of the energy behind complementarianism and the search for "clear gender roles" comes from a crisis of masculinity. Instead of digging deeper into Scripture for guidance about how women and men can live as disciples who conform to Christ, the masculinity movement offers cheap and superficial answers, which end up ruining men and their relationships.

The Christian masculinity movement isn't helping men or women. It's damaging young men and their relationships with others, and it's distracting us from what should be our proper focus—discipleship and imitating Christ. Good discipleship based on a correct understanding of the gospel calls us to challenge gender roles in dating, marriage, church, and society.

Young men are looking for guidance on how to live well and relate to each other and women. But a hyper-focus on "masculinity" or "femininity" as the pinnacle of discipleship does not help. We need to guide men and women toward honoring, respecting, and relating to each other as equal partners and coheirs with Christ. The church can do this well by helping both men and women become disciples who imitate Christ Jesus. For men (and women), this means helping them discover how they can become fully conformed to Christ, pursuing lives characterized by virtue and the fruit of the Spirit (Gal. 5:22–23). Shifting our focus away from masculinity or femininity to focus on conformity to the image of Christ would go a long way toward helping us all break free of harmful gender theology.

When our churches make this shift, some will ask, "Are you saying you don't think that the differences between women and men are biblical?" This is a challenging question. On the one hand, the Bible does not deny that there are differences between women and men but discerning the nature of these differences isn't straightforward (and gender roles vary from culture to culture and generation to generation). On the other hand, the

Bible isn't focused on "masculinity" or "femininity." So, when we make the nature of gender our focus, we quickly fall into the trap of mirroring worldly ideas of manhood and womanhood. When we focus on "biblical manhood" or "biblical womanhood," our eyes are on the wrong thing. Healthy personal identity grows when we focus on discipleship and conformity to Christ. And when we focus on this kind of discipleship, we also foster healthy relationships between the sexes.

So, if we aren't talking to boys and men about "Christian masculinity" or "biblical manhood" anymore, what guidance are we giving them? How are we helping them form personal identities and flourish as men? Thankfully, we already have some guides available.

Recently, a major men's conference was held in our city (Sydney). The keynote speaker offered three talks on what a man of faith should look like. The speaker asserted that a man should be:

1. Fearless, standing in awe of God and allowing who he is to lead us into living fearlessly.
2. Tender, reflecting the justice, kindness, and humility of God.
3. Thankful, recognizing all God has done for us in Christ.

This sounds like a beautiful description of discipleship. But it also sounds like a perfect description of a woman of faith. When we see that discipleship is about conformity to Christ regardless of gender, we will see how virtues apply to everyone.

We should notice, also, that when the biblical authors give guidance to men and women about how to relate to each other, their advice isn't a focus on "masculinity" or "femininity." Their guidance could be summarized like this: Practice mutual submission and honor one another. Understand that you are equal partners and co-laborers with your brothers and sisters. Together, you are coheirs with your brother, Jesus Christ. Live together in a way that witnesses Christ and his gospel and maintains the credibility of your witness in an age of unbelief, persecution, immorality, enslavement, and patriarchy. Be attentive to the expectations and norms of your culture—you can't give constant offense and maintain credible witness. But never sacrifice conformity to Christ, your gospel witness, or mutual submission. In your relationships with each other, imitate Christ's love, grace, compassion, gentleness, kindness, humility, self-sacrifice, and so on. Live as a new creation, as a new people in Christ Jesus. In every aspect of your relationships together as women and men, seek to glorify Christ and be conformed to his image until he returns.

Healthy personal identity and interpersonal wellbeing develop as we help boys and men live as disciples who conform to the image of Jesus Christ. Disciples like this practice gender equality, mutual submission, and self-sacrificial nurture and honor of others. Only this leads to healthy disciples, churches, marriages, and ministries.

God became a vulnerable and humble human in the incarnation. Jesus Christ uniquely understands our humanity, and he sacrificed himself for us. That's the scandal of the cross. Jesus is the suffering and crucified servant. He invites us into a life of humility and vulnerability and sacrifice. We follow a vulnerable Messiah, and we must imitate his weakness and his humility. Our aim should be to help men and women understand that a cruciform faith embraces suffering, self-emptying, and vulnerability. In doing so, the humble disciple discovers the power of the cross and resurrection and lives in a manner pleasing to God.

The most significant threats to Christianity today aren't immigration, same-sex marriage, or increasing secularism in Western countries. The greatest dangers to Christianity today are greed, pride, idolatry, selfishness, and abuse of power, along with a combative posture in the world, which fears and excludes others. The answer to these problems is to move from fear and exclusion to discipleship and conformity to Jesus Christ. This is everything. From this posture flows the integrity, morality, values, compassion, humility, love, and witness the world needs. The Christian masculinity movement can't do that—only discipleship can.

God predestined his people to be conformed to the image of his Son (Rom. 8:29). Our major difficulty isn't gendered roles or lack of "biblical manhood." Our great challenge is our lack of conformity to the image of Christ. Discipleship and conformity go hand in glove. They're inseparable. We don't need more masculine or feminine Christians; we need more disciples. Today, perhaps more than ever, our focus should be on discipleship and conformity to the image of Christ. It's time to challenge unhealthy gender roles and stereotypes. Let's stop talking about "masculinity" and "femininity"—let's talk about discipleship.[29]

Biola University research among two hundred and sixteen Protestant Christian churchgoers found "that individuals with higher levels of Authoritarianism, Conservatism, Traditionalism, Social Dominance Orientation, Hostile Sexism, and Benevolent Sexism prefer biblical interpretations that endorse gender hierarchy."[30] The correlation between power and sexism and forms of biblical interpretation that preference gender hierarchy is perhaps not surprising, but it is disturbing. The researchers conclude:

> Goldstein (1960) hypothesized that Christian theology is often representative of men's experiences, and attention to the female experience will likely yield alternative views of Scripture. This study provides support to Goldstein's hypothesis by showing that men and women have a tendency to interpret passages in the Bible differently. Furthermore, their different perspectives on Scripture are related to their social attitudes and beliefs, which are likely shaped by their different social-contextual experiences, especially those related to Traditionalism. Therefore, these results highlight the importance of gaining a female perspective in Scripture interpretation.[31]

Australian church leaders must stand with their Asian Australian sisters as the church, collectively, amplifies the voices and contributions of these women and pushes back against hierarchical and oppressive notions of masculinity and femininity and

---

29. Hill, "Let's Stop Talking."
30. Orme et al., "Power, Sexism," 274.
31. Orme et al., "Power, Sexism," 282–83.

unbiblical gender roles and expectations. Asian Australian women and their allies can occasionally look to biblical figures for inspiration in this quest.

Ciin Sian Siam Hatzaw turns to Esther, for instance, in this pursuit. She writes that it's possible to interpret Esther:

> ... in light of her marginalized identity. Her position as a Jewish woman in diaspora who must hide her ethnicity and assimilate into Persian culture reveals parallels to contemporary Asian women in Western diaspora, due to perpetuated stereotypes of passiveness and submission, and the model minority myth associated with Asian immigration. Esther's sexualization reveals further parallels to the fetishization and sexual exploitation of Asian women. If we read the text in light of her marginalization, we can highlight the racial and gendered oppression within the existing power structures, as well as the levels of privilege at work within the character dynamics. Esther serves as an example of the potential that lies in recognising positions of privilege, the implications of identity, and understanding different forms of resistance in order to form a liberative theology. [My work] outlines the position of Asian women and their proximity to whiteness in relation to other BIPOC (black, indigenous, and people of colour) communities, revealing unexpected connections to Esther's character ... Through her story, Asian women in diaspora may find their experiences reflected in the journey to liberation.[32]

Honoring the vitality and worth of the theology, mission, and ministry of Asian Australian women goes hand in glove with dismantling damaging, hierarchical, colonial images of masculinity, femininity, and race.

---

32. Hatzaw Ciin Sian, "Reading Esther," 1. For examples of how Asian Australian women are challenging various aspects of "national" Australian culture, see Carole, "Preoccupations."

FAR HORIZONS

CHALLENGING THE SINS AND MYOPIA OF AUSTRALIAN SOCIETY

Australian Christian leaders must join with Asian Australian women, Aboriginal and Torres Strait Islander peoples, and marginalized groups in naming and challenging the sins and myopia of Australian church and society. These sins take many forms, perpetuate injustice and discrimination, and include racism, sexism, ableism, ageism, and classism.

The Australian church is complicit in Australia's foundational sin. Brooke Prentis is a Wakka Wakka woman, Aboriginal Christian leader, and CEO of Common Grace. She says that the original sin of the Australian nation "is the theft of the land, and that's something that hasn't been dealt with."[33] Many injustices have followed our original sin, including "stolen land, stolen wages, stolen lives, the failure to close the gap, overrepresentation in prison systems, Aboriginal children in Northern Territory detention centers, and the destruction of sacred sites."[34]

In addition to our shameful treatment of our Indigenous peoples, racism is more pervasive in Australian society than many Australians like to acknowledge. In 2021, the Lowy Institute released research called "Being Chinese in Australia," and the Scanlon Foundation published a study titled the "Mapping Social Cohesion Report." Both reports found significant anti-Asian racism in Australia, with substantial numbers of Asian Australians being threatened or attacked in the previous twelve months, and especially since the rise of the Covid pandemic.[35]

Sexism continues to be a problem in the Australian church and society. Our leaders too often turn a blind eye to it. The plague

---

33. Toh, "Original Sins."
34. Toh, "Original Sins."
35. Tan et al., " Measure of Prejudice; Kassam and Hsu, *Being Chinese in Australia*; Markus, *Mapping Social Cohesion*. Many studies have also examined racism within Australia's educational institutions and the need for more diversity and interculturality among students, staff, faculty, and administrators. See, for example, Allen, "Creative Diversity."

of sexism permeates all levels of Australian society. As the Australian Institute of International Affairs notes:

> Australia has yet again made international headlines for the toxic sexist culture of its federal parliament. The recent ABC Four Corners episode, Inside The Canberra Bubble, exposed a history of sexism and inappropriate behavior by senior members of the coalition government . . . They have thrust Australia's sexist political culture, yet again, into the international spotlight. The New York Times quickly covered these new examples of sexism, describing Australia as "a step or ten behind . . . many of its developed peers," where politicians are willing "to let government institutions be run like gentleman's clubs of yesteryear."[36]

Seventeen years ago, Julia Baird wrote a book about the media, women, and politics in Australia. Here's what she observed in 2004 when she wrote *Media Tarts: How the Australian Press Frames Female Politicians*.

> Trawling through decades of clippings files, I found that the media repeatedly framed female politicians in ways that made them seem interlopers and that made their exercise of authority seem peculiar and unnatural. The dominant tropes I found were: the Housewife (Can you pose doing the washing, the dishes, or the vacuuming? And assure readers you are a "real, relatable" woman?); the Steel Sheila (A woman doing a competent job or making unpopular decisions must be made of metal! A freak!); the Cover Girl (Can you pose in this bikini while accepting your trivialization?); the Feminine Feminist (She speaks of equality but, importantly, still looks pretty and seems nice); and the Sinning Saint (How dare a dainty woman do politics like the men? Be ambitious, gather numbers, make mistakes?)[37])

Citing some shameful recent examples of misogyny against female Australian public leaders and figures, Julia Baird describes

---

36. Williams, "Toxic Sexist Culture."
37. Baird, "What's Changed." See Baird, *Media Tarts*.

how Australian society continues to display sexism. But Julia observes that we may be "finally witnessing a tipping point," where women are going public about their experiences of sexual harassment, bullying, and misogyny, and where what once was overlooked is now being called out. "But for too long, so many women MPs, like Victorian children, have been seen but not heard."[38]

Many Australian Christians and churches address these injustices and wrongs with courage and passion. However, until the broader Australian church sees and owns its complicity in racism, sexism, and the abuse of our First Nations peoples, we will not be able to testify to the justice, mercy, and shalom of God. The voices of our Asian Australian sisters and Indigenous peoples cry out. Will we listen, repent, and change?

THE END OF WHITE MALE CHRISTIAN AUSTRALIA

The NCLS 2016 data (which surveyed 21,987 Asian Australian Christian women), the thirty-six in-depth surveys (five of which were Asian American women for the sake of comparison), and the fifteen interviews provide rich data on the experiences of Asian Australian women in mission and ministry. These women come from various Asian ethnicities and cultures, a broad range of theological and denominational traditions (Protestant, Evangelical, Catholic, Pentecostal, and more), and from first and second generations. The women come from all the major cities of Australia and from rural, regional, and urban areas. Their experiences span local church ministry, local and global missions, and ministry in other Christian organizations.

The NCLS 2016 offers insight into the values and ministries of 21,987 Asian Australian women. Our thirty-six surveys and fifteen interviews allowed us to dive deeper into the experiences of Asian Australian women serving in mission and ministry. There are benefits to considering an extensive quantitative data set like the NCLS 2016 with a smaller group of qualitative surveys and interviews.

---

38. Baird, "What's Changed."

The first gives the researcher a broad snapshot, while the second allows one to dig deeper into a group's experiences and perspectives.

This study allowed us to reflect briefly on a range of essential questions. What theological and missiological themes perpetuate or challenge the suppression of Asian Australian women in mission and ministry? What relevant ecclesial shifts are happening in Australian churches that Australian Christians can no longer ignore? What roles do Asian Australian women play in ministry and mission (including evangelism, mission, community service, social justice, and welfare)? What are their attitudes to ministry, mission, service, evangelism, welfare, and social justice? What are their experiences of inequality, power, discrimination, vulnerability, and woundedness in ministry and mission? Why should the church focus on releasing these women to mission and ministry? How can we address racism, sexism, and inequalities?

It is important to note that the inequalities, experiences, systemic racism and injustices, and cultural and gender expectations revealed in the interviews will have influenced the NCLS 2016 results. It is too easy, for instance, to jump to misleading conclusions about what Asian Australian women value without (1) considering the diversity of women in this group, and (2) considering how injustices, expectations, cultures, and other factors influenced the answers these women gave to the NCLS 2016 questions.

This investigation requires further work and future research. There is a need to investigate further the views, theologies, and experiences of Asian Australian women from particular ethnicities and theological traditions and compare them with each other. Chinese women's experiences and perspectives in Reformed Evangelical churches are not the same as Filipino women in Catholic churches, for example. First and second generations view things differently, too. This study, therefore, has had limitations we have named here. This investigation is a starting point for more comprehensive and particularized examinations and research.

Australian churches, denominations, mission agencies, and Christian organizations and not-for-profits must recognize, nurture, and amplify the voices and gifts of Asian Australian women. There are those in such Christian organizations that question whether women can be successful leaders. But as Graham highlighted in *Holding Up Half the Sky*, the latest research into leadership effectiveness across a wide range of secular, corporate, religious, and not-for-profit organizations shows the opposite. Women lead effectively. The research indicates that by many measures, they lead better than men. In *Scaling Research*, Robert J. Anderson and William A. Adams draw on decades of research into leadership effectiveness among Fortune 500 companies and government agencies. They conclude the following about female leadership after examining the quality research and data:

> To summarize, this data suggests that *women lead more effectively than men*. Since we see a strong positive correlation between Leadership Effectiveness and Creative Competency scores, we conclude that women are more effective because they tend to lead more Creatively and less Reactively. Women leaders are more Creative, more effective, and tend to get better results than men. The predominance of relationship strengths in the Top 10 list suggests that *women are more effective because they lead more relationally*. Doing so also requires a high degree of self-awareness and authenticity.[39]

The center and heart of Christianity aren't among the powerful and privileged, including white male leaders and theologians. The end of white male Christian Australia has finally arrived. Rosemary Radford Ruether asserts:

> Christ goes particularly to the outcasts, and they, in turn, have a special affinity for the gospel. But the aim of this partiality is to create a new whole. To elevate the valleys and make the high places low, so that all may come into a new place of God's reign, when God's will is done on earth . . . If one can say Christ comes to the oppressed and the oppressed especially hear him, then it is women from these marginal groups who are often seen as both the oppressed of the oppressed and also as those particularly receptive to the gospel . . . Jesus as liberator calls

---

39. Hill, *Holding Up Half the Sky*, xxii. Anderson and Adams, *Scaling Leadership*, 7.

for the renunciation and dissolution of the web of status relations by which societies have defined privilege and unprivileged. He speaks especially to outcast women, not as representatives of the "feminine," but because they are at the bottom of the network of oppression. His ability to be liberator does not reside in his maleness, but on the contrary, in the fact that he has renounced this system of domination and seeks to embody in his person the new humanity of service and mutual empowerment.[40]

In *The End of White Christian America*, Robert P. Jones shows how many of the most heated debates in North America—such as same-sex marriage, religious liberty, undocumented migrants, political partisanship, the abuses within the justice system—can only be adequately understood and examined "in the context of the anxieties that white Christians feel as the racial, religious, and cultural landscape has changed around them."[41]

One could make the same argument in the Australian context. The most controversial issues in Australian church and society relate directly to how white, European-derived Australian Christians and other traditional white sub-cultures feel about changes to Australian culture. These changes include cultural diversity, religious pluralism, and secularized institutions. Jones says there is much at stake in whether these white Christians "retreat into disengaged enclaves, band together to launch repeated rounds of what the sociologist Nathan Glazer has called 'defensive offensives'—in which a formerly powerful majority recasts itself as a beleaguered minority in an attempt to preserve its particular social values—or find a way to integrate [into the new cultural landscape]."[42]

White male Christian Australia is dying. For many, this death is filled with grief and loss. For some, there is a desire to return to an imagined and idealized Christendom past. For those oppressed and marginalized, this past was filled with suffering, misogyny, racism, and pain. For many, this death of white male Christian Australia "is a cause for considerable grief; for others, relief or even celebration.

40. Ruether, *To Change the World*, 53–56.
41. Jones, *White Christian America*. Dust Jacket.
42. Jones, *White Christian America*, 43–44.

But this much is clear: in the soil fertilized by White Christian America's remains [and white male Christian Australia's remnants], new life is taking root."[43]

The end of white male Christian Australia is near. Will the Australian church and its congregations and leaders listen and learn from those who have been marginalized? Will we open our hearts and minds to those who tell us stories of injustice, silencing, and discrimination? Will we find ways to be a people of justice, equality, mercy, and peace in a politically, religiously, and culturally diverse Australia? Asian Australian women, Aboriginal and Torres Strait Islanders, and marginalized groups can guide us into this far horizon of fresh hope and new life.

43. Jones, *White Christian America*, 239.

Afterword by Grace Ji-Sun Kim

In 2019, I had the privilege of traveling to Australia with my daughter to preach, speak, and participate in a book launch for *Healing Our Broken Humanity*, co-written with Graham Joseph Hill. During that visit, Graham showed us some of the most serene beaches and breathtaking mountains of Australia. The beauty of the people and the natural land made it one of the most memorable trips of my life. To have done it with my daughter was a great privilege of mine.

During the trip, Graham provided us with a short history of Australia. I found the history of migration fascinating. Much like America, besides the Aboriginal peoples, everyone else that settled in Australia is an immigrant. Some were convicts. Today, immigration continues to take place, but with most of the movement coming from Asia. The increase of the Asian population in Australia will only continue to grow. It is crucial to investigate the cultural and societal impact immigration makes on Australian society. Furthermore, it is essential to understand how these immigrant Asian churches are engaged in ministry and how Asian women can have flourishing ministries in Australia.

Graham Joseph Hill and Jessie Giyou Kim's book, *Sunburnt Country, Sweeping Pains*, is a significant contribution to deepening our knowledge of Asian Australian women's experiences and how they are engaging with and contributing to ministry. Asian immigrants in Australia experience racism, marginalization, and

Afterword by Grace Ji-Sun Kim

discrimination from the dominant white society, as they do in many other places such as the United States. They are victims of myths such as being honorific whites or the model minority, which attempts to diminish their experiences of marginality and discrimination with the supposed notions of economic and academic success—tangential or ascendant to whites—allowing their experiences of racism to be undermined. In such a context, it becomes especially difficult for Asian Australian women who experience sexism and racism to voice their stories and find status as leaders within and outside their ethnic communities.

Asian Australian women live under limiting restrictions of patriarchy found in the white Australian society and their Asian communities. As described in this book, patriarchy is deeply embedded in Asian churches and profoundly affects Asian Australian women. Confucianism and its long patriarchal traditions are part of Asian cultures, societies, and religious life. This seeps into Christian faith communities as patriarchy is a significant part of the fabric of the church. Since patriarchy is deeply embedded in the life of the church and faith communities, it will take courage and determination to dismantle it and work towards a just and equitable church. The change will also require the communal effort of the church as a global institution. In this effort, Asian Australian women live in hope: hope given by Christ to those who hear and follow his word; hope that inspires and sustains; and hope that supports and guides in the effort to live by justice and establish equity in the *Sunburnt Country*.

Grace Ji-Sun Kim
Professor of Theology, Earlham School of Religion
Richmond, Indiana, USA

Appendix 1

21 Asian Australian Women Leaders and Theologians You Should Know

The quality of leadership and scholarship among Asian Australian Christian women is outstanding. We are privileged to call many of these women friends. Here are twenty-one Asian Australian women leaders and theologians you should know.

AMELIA KOH-BUTLER

Dr. Amelia Koh-Butler is a Chinese-Scottish-Aussie, with connections to Adnyamathanha country in the Ikara-Flinders. As World Methodist Council's Worship and Liturgy Convenor, she has taught in North and Central America, Italy, France, Spain, Korea, Thailand, and Singapore. Previous graduate studies in music, creative arts, theology, and education, led to intercultural doctoral research through Fuller (Pasadena) in integrated Missiology, Ethnomusicology, and Fresh Expressions of Church.

Currently Minister at Eastwood Multilingual Uniting Church, Amelia Koh-Butler was part of teams introducing ministry innovations to Australia: Walk to Emmaus, Godly Play, and Mission-Shaped Ministry. She served as Executive Director of UC Mission Resourcing in South Australia, Multi-Faith Chaplain at Western Sydney University, and Minister at Wesley, Newcastle.

APPENDIX 1

She was Director of Lay Education (ELM) in the Uniting Church in NSW and ACT.

Publications include *Must Have Experience* (with Ross Neville, 2004), *Peacemaking and Discipleship* (with Chris Walker, MediaCom), *Wide and Deep* (liturgical resources, 2016, Mediacom), *Sisters in Scripture* (evocations, 2017, MediaCom), and contributed to the 2020 collection from Stephen Burns and Robert Gribben, "*When We Pray*." She co-authored (with Rev. Dr. Tony Floyd) the *Space for Grace* (2011–2019) process for intercultural theological discernment, used by the Uniting Church and explored by members of the World Methodist Church and World Council of Churches.

Amelia Koh-Butler is a foundation member of Scriptural Reasoning (Muslim-Christian scholars in interfaith dialogue about sacred texts) and the Uniting Church in Australia National Advocate for Ecumenical and Interfaith Relations.

CAROLYN E. L. TAN

Dr. Carolyn E. L. Tan's background is Singaporean-Malaysian, and she worked as a pediatric surgeon in Singapore until 2005. Discerning God's call to theological studies, she moved to Perth, Western Australia, enrolling in the Baptist Theological College of Western Australia (renamed Vose Seminary in 2009). Having graduated with the Master of Divinity, Carolyn was encouraged to undertake theological research. This culminated in a doctorate and the publication of her thesis in the Australian College of Theology monograph series in 2019 (*The Spirit at the Cross: Exploring a Cruciform Pneumatology*).

The compelling question that God placed before Carolyn in her research was this: "What was the Holy Spirit's role at the cross of Jesus Christ?" Was the Spirit present and active during the most important moment in the history of humanity's redemption, or was the Spirit passively waiting until the Son had finished his task? Could the Son have completed his redemptive mission without the Holy Spirit's involvement? In this regard, what clues may we glean from the New Testament, and what have Christian scholars, through the centuries, thought about this question? Does the Holy Spirit's redemptive role only begin with the resurrection of Jesus Christ? Carolyn believes that her considerations and reflections are only part of an ongoing conversation about the work of the Holy Spirit. Just as she has benefited enormously from the prior work of others, she hopes that more will continue to explore the height, depth, and breadth of the Spirit's role in redemption and consider its significance for our understanding of the person and work of the Holy Spirit.

CRISTINA LLEDO GOMEZ

Dr. Cristina Lledo Gomez is a Systematic Theologian and the Presentation Sisters Lecturer at BBI—The Australian Institute of Theological Education (TAITE). She is also a Religion and Society Research Fellow at Charles Sturt University's Public and Contextual Theology Research Centre (PACT).

Cristina Lledo Gomez received her Master of Theology at the Catholic Institute of Sydney and her PhD in Theology at Charles Sturt University. Her current role at BBI—TAITE is directed towards promoting women's spiritualities, feminist theologies, and ecotheologies. Her first book was *The Church as Woman and Mother: Historical and Theological Foundations*, published in 2018. Currently, she is co-editing *The God of Interruption: Mothering and Theology*, and writing her second monograph, *A Babayi Theology from Australia: Embracing a Maternal-Feminist Indigenous Heritage for Filipinas.*

In 2015 to 2016, Cristina Lledo Gomez was the Visiting International Research Fellow for Boston College's School of Theology and Ministry, and in 2020 she was the Catherine Mowry Lacugna Awardee for New Scholars for her essay "Mother Language, Mother Church, Mother Earth," conferred by the Catholic Theological Society of America.

Cristina Lledo Gomez has served on boards and committees, including the first lay Chair of the Australian Catholic Social Justice Council (2019–2020), Chair for the Committee for Underrepresented Ethnic Groups (2018–2021) at the Catholic Theological

Society of America, and currently Board Member-at-Large for the Ecclesiological Investigations Network (2019–present).

Cristina is wife to Adrian and mother to Sophia and Julian.

ENQI WENG

Dr. Enqi Weng is a media scholar and sociologist of religion. She completed her PhD in the School of Media and Communications at RMIT University in 2018 and has since published her monograph *Media Perceptions of Religious Changes in Australia: Of Dominance and Diversity* (Routledge, 2020). Her doctoral thesis analyzed media representation of religions in Australia and revealed that public discussions about religion were not only primarily constructed and influenced by white male perspectives, British influences also problematically continued to be integral in shaping these discussions in postcolonial Australia. Her research interest has since turned towards decolonial/multicultural approaches to the sociological study of religion, where her work interrogates the role that news media plays in reinforcing and normalizing the racialization of religion. She is currently a Research Fellow at the Alfred Deakin Institute for Citizenship and Globalization at Deakin University. Occasionally she teaches across media and religious studies units at Deakin. She was born and raised in Singapore, grew up nonreligious and into spirituality, and came to Christ in her early twenties. She has lived in Melbourne since 2010, and her lived experiences in Anglo-majority churches also informed her research perspective.

Selected recent publications include:

> Weng, Enqi, et al. "Whiteness, Religious Diversity and Relational Belonging: Opportunities and Challenges for the New African Diaspora in Australia." *Journal for the Academic Study of Religion*, forthcoming.
>
> Weng, Enqi, and Alexandra Wake. "Blessed be the Educated Journalist: Reflections on a Religious Literacy Gap in the Field of Journalism." *Australian Journalism Review* 43, no. 1 (2021) 81–97.

Weng, Enqi, and Fethi Mansouri. "'Swamped by Muslims' and Facing an 'African Gang' Problem: Racialized and Religious Media Representations in Australia." *Continuum*: Journal of Media and Cultural Studies (2021), 1–19.

Weng, Enqi. "Christianity in Contemporary Australian Media: 'Get Your Rosaries Off My Ovaries.'" In *Grounded in the Body, in Time and Place, in Scripture*, edited by Jill Firth and Denise Cooper-Clarke, 219–234. Eugene OR: Wipf & Stock, 2021.

GEMMA TULUD CRUZ

Dr. Gemma Tulud Cruz is a Filipino-Australian theologian who completed her doctoral studies in theology in the Netherlands. She taught for several years in the United States before moving to Australia. She is currently Senior Lecturer in the School of Theology at Australian Catholic University, where she has also served as Course Coordinator for Postgraduate Studies. Gemma is affiliated with ACU's Institute of Religion and Critical Inquiry. She is former Vice-President for Australia for ANZATS (Australia and New Zealand Association of Theological Schools) and serves on the editorial board of a couple of peer-reviewed journals. She has also been involved at the national level with the Catholic Church in Australia, particularly as a member of the Council for Australian Catholic Women (CACW), the Executive Committee for the Plenary Council, and the Australian Catholic Social Justice Council.

Gemma Tulud Cruz has delivered endowed public lectures and conference keynote and plenary addresses in Australia, Europe, North America, and Asia. She is the author of numerous publications, particularly on theologies of migration. These include *Christianity Across Borders: Theology and Contemporary Issues in Global Migration* (Routledge, 2021) and *Toward a Theology of Migration: Social Justice and Religious Experience* (Palgrave Macmillan, 2014).

APPENDIX 1

GRACE LUNG

Grace Lung's passion is restoring brokenness in cultural communities to Jesus through contextualizing the gospel to Asian Australians and developing Asian churches in Australia. Grace is a graduate of Sydney Missionary and Bible College and Fuller Theological Seminary and is currently doing postgraduate studies through Stirling Theological College.

Grace Lung was an Anglican Deaconess Ministries Summer Fellow in 2019. Her writing has appeared in SOLA Network, the Gospel Coalition Australia, Ethos (EA Centre for Christianity and Society), and Centered: Resources for the Asian American Church. In her current roles, she serves on the pastoral staff at Brisbane Chinese Alliance Church, works with the Centre of Asian Christianity at the Brisbane School of Theology, hosts a podcast "Did You Eat Yet?" with the RICE Movement, and serves on OMF QLD's Ministry Team. Grace has produced the *Asians Between Cultures* course, which helps faith leaders in Asian contexts discover how understanding the gospel with both ethnicity and faith can transform their ministry and relationships. Her website is gracelung.com.

GRACE KWAN SIK TSOI

Dr. Grace Kwan Sik Tsoi was born in Hong Kong and migrated to Australia with her family during high school. She studied at the University of New South Wales and was awarded a BSc (Med), and MBBS. Upon graduation, she was called to full-time ministry, so she left the medical field, entered seminary studies, and was awarded a BTh (Hons) from Sydney College of Divinity. She pastored the Chinese Congregation of Canberra Chinese Christian Church from 2009 to 2015 and was ordained in 2013.

Grace Kwan Sik Tsoi received a PhD from the University of Divinity (Whitley College) in 2019, and her thesis is forthcoming in print under the title "Who Is To Blame for Judges 19? Interplay Between the Text and a Chinese Context." She began teaching in the Chinese Theological College Australia in 2019 and is currently the Academic Dean and lecturer for Old Testament studies. Her research interest includes narrative criticism, intertextuality, ideological criticism, and contextual criticism.

HANNA HYUN

Dr. Hanna Hyun has researched Muslim diasporas settled in pluralistic societies in the United States and Australia. She completed her PhD in Intercultural Studies at Reformed Theological Seminary in Jackson, Mississippi, served as an assistant professor at Kosin University in 2013 to 2015, and worked at Sydney College of Divinity from 2016 to 2020.

Hanna Hyun currently serves as an adjunct professor at Juan International University and has held the position of director of the Centre for Islamic Studies in Sydney since 2018. Her main research areas include, but are not limited to, the following areas: Islamic Studies, Migration Theology, Studies of Diasporas and Refugees, Multicultural Church Planting, and Women in Mission.

JESSICA COLLINS

Jessica Collins was born at the coal face of mission life. As the daughter of second-generation missionaries, she was born in Lamma Island, Hong Kong—a once quiet fishing village that has become the central hub for many ex-pats worldwide. Throughout her young life, she accompanied her parents and grandparents into the Southeast Asian mission field. She was no stranger to Thailand, Myanmar, the Philippines, and Hong Kong, training and raising disciples wherever they went.

In a youth camp at age thirteen, Jessica Collins heard God tell her to devote her life to ministry, which became the motivating force of her adult life. In her twenties, she moved to Chiang Mai, Thailand, and taught in a discipleship training school, equipping locals to bring the gospel into some of the most war-torn parts of the Myanmar border. Years later, God drew her to a church nestled within the red-light districts of Hong Kong. In an economically disparate area, with wealthy Chinese migrants residing amongst

APPENDIX 1

locals in poverty, Jess pastored the youth and assisted in social welfare programs.

In 2018, Jessica Collins took on Steward of the Online Bible College, a digital Bible college established more than two decades earlier by her late father to equip people with in-depth teaching of the word of God. At present, Jess is a devoted mother of two beautiful girls. She lives in Western Sydney with her husband, Peter, and is an Associate Pastor at Epping Church of Christ which strives to be a thriving all-age, cross-cultural church.

Jessica Collins now equips more than 50,000 students worldwide registered to the Online Bible College, stewarding the platform in an ever-evolving technological age and growing physical campuses in Thailand, Myanmar, and the United States.

JESSIE GIYOU KIM

Jessie Giyou Kim graduated with a Bachelor of Theology through the Australian College of Theology. She serves in ministry at a Baptist Church in Sydney. Jessie was born in Seoul, South Korea, and moved to China at age fifteen. Jessie has served in missions in China, Australia, Cambodia, and Vietnam. Her areas of interest include mission, children's ministry, and caring for people. She is pursuing ordination for pastoral ministry with the Baptist Churches of Australia to become a pastor and missionary.

Jessie Giyou Kim grew up in various parts of Asia and is fluent in Chinese, Korean, and English. Jessie Giyou Kim supported research for this book and TheGlobalChurchProject.com by researching Asian and Asian diaspora theologians and translating publications into Chinese and Korean.

JUSTINE TOH

Dr. Justine Toh is Senior Fellow at the Centre for Public Christianity. She speaks and writes about the Christian faith and contemporary life in publications like the *Sydney Morning Herald*, *The Canberra Times*, *The Spectator*, *ABC Online*, and *ABC Religion & Ethics*. She occasionally guest hosts ABC RN's *God Forbid*, a panel program exploring contemporary religion, and has co-presented the documentary *For the Love of God: How the Church Is Better and Worse Than You Ever Imagined*.

Justine Toh has a PhD in Cultural Studies from Macquarie University in Sydney. She is the author of *Achievement Addiction* that explores, among other things, the harms and the economic necessity of "tiger parenting" as well as the spiritual fallout of living in a world obsessed with achievement. Justine also tweets, erratically, at @justinetoh.

MIRIAM CHAN

Miriam Chan is a returned missionary mother and remains passionate about missions and being a mother to her two elementary-aged children. Since returning to Sydney, Australia, she has worked with a mission agency in preparing others to serve cross-culturally. She enjoys wearing multiple hats during the week as a university counselor, ministry wife, Cavoodle-lover, and Sunday school teacher.

Miriam Chan and Sophia Russell co-edited *For the Joy: 21 Missionary Mother Stories of Real Life and Faith* (William Carey, 2019).

MONICA JYOTSNA MELANCHTHON

Dr. Monica Jyotsna Melanchthon is a Lutheran raised in an ecumenical environment. The Andhra Evangelical Lutheran Church ordained her in India in 2009. A graduate of the United Theological College, Bangalore, and the Lutheran School of Theology at Chicago, she has been teaching Hebrew Bible studies at Pilgrim Theological College, University of Divinity, Melbourne, since June 2012 after having served on the faculty of the Gurukul Lutheran Theological College, Chennai, for seventeen years.

Monica Jyotsna Melanchthon positions herself as a feminist advocate and a liberation theologian, committed to producing reflections and texts that resist countercultures and languages

Appendix 1

of dominance that exclude the voices of the oppressed. She has published in various academic books focusing primarily on interpretations of OT texts from the perspective of the Indian context and the marginalized. Her approach to the biblical text is critical, contextual, interdisciplinary, and liberative. She draws on insights from the marginalized's lived experiences and social biographies, particularly women and Dalits, to interpret the biblical text.

Monica Jyotsna Melanchthon is an active member of the Society of Biblical Literature and sits on its council. She is also the President of the Society of Asian Biblical Studies, committed to fostering biblical studies in Asia with attention to the Asian context. She is currently on the editorial boards of *JFSR*, *Bible and Critical Theory*, and on the advisory council of *Word & World: Theology for Christian Ministry*. Over the years, she has resourced the wider church both locally and internationally as speaker and Bible study leader and through involvement in study projects and conferences of the LWF and the CWM.

Some of her forthcoming books and essays include:

> *Terror in the Bible: Rhetoric, Gender, and Violence*, edited by Monica J. Melanchthon and Robyn Whitaker (SBL, forthcoming)

> *Bible Blindspots: Dispersion and Othering*, edited by Jione Havea and Monica J. Melanchthon (Wipf and Stock, 2021)

> "Reading for Justice, Dignity and Life: Feminist Interpretations of the Hebrew Bible in South Asia." In *A Textbook on Asian Feminist Biblical Studies*, edited by Kwok Pui-Lan and Maggie Low (Chinese University of Hong Kong, 2021)

> "Gender, Violence, and the Dalit Psyche: The Jephthah Story Reconsidered (Judges 11 & 12)." In *Terror in the Bible: Rhetoric, Gender, and Violence*, edited by Monica Jyotsna Melanchthon and Robyn Whitaker (SBL, 2021)

> "Women and Masculinity: Hindu India and Second Temple Judah." In *Bible Blindspots: Dispersion and Othering*, edited by Jione Havea and Monica J. Melanchthon (Wipf and Stock, 2021)

"Shifting and Shrewd Lutheran Identities: Reflections from Asia." In *Blessed are the Peacemakers: Theology, Compassion and Action for a Global Mission: Essays in Honour of Munib Younan*, edited by Munther Isaac and Maria Leppäkari (Luther-Agricola-Seura, 2021).

Monica Jyotsna Melanchthon's most recent publications include "John 12:1–8: Reflections," *In God's Image: Journal of Asian Women's Resource Centre for Culture and Theology* 39 (2020) 104–12; "Rape Matters: Dinah (Genesis 34) Meets Asifa Bano," in *Vulnerability and Resilience: Body and Liberating Theologies*, edited by Jione Havea, 89–103 (Lexington, 2020); "Teaching Biblical Studies in a Pandemic—India," *Journal of Biblical Literature* 139, no. 3 (2020) 613–18 (with Mothy Varkey); and "Making Connections: Dinah, Luther and Indian Women," in *The Alternative Luther: Lutheran Theology from the Subaltern*, edited by Else Marie-Wiberg Petersen ,195–214 (Lexington/Fortress, 2019).

NAOMI CHONG

Naomi Chong leads the RICE Movement with her husband, Steve, as a platform to catalyze and mobilize a generation for the kingdom. The RICE Movement works primarily with second-generation Asian youth and young adults, gathering to equip and empower them to share the gospel and live out the kingdom in all spheres of life. This movement has had a significant impact in the Global South and is spreading rapidly worldwide in major cities where Asians congregate.

Naomi seeks to empower a generation of women by addressing cultural and systemic impediments to healthy biblical identity as daughters of God and coheirs of the kingdom.

A proponent for justice, Naomi has been invited by Micah Australia as one of forty women leaders across Australia to represent Christian leaders to advocate for social justice issues in the South Pacific.

Appendix 1

More of a practitioner than a theologian, Naomi's various iterations have been studying and working as an arts and law graduate, pursuing mission work overseas, doing a ministry apprenticeship, working as a youth worker in a church, and studying a bachelor's degree in theology. She then went on to church planting, motherhood, and now leading a movement. Naomi's desire has constantly been to see the lost saved. She loves God's word and prayer. As a couple, she and her husband Steve continuously pursue radical faith in action, epitomized in a bold trip to minister just ten kilometers outside ISIS headquarters in Iraq, among the persecuted church. They have a growing heart for mission, especially into Asia, and are enjoying this season of unprecedented God-given acceleration in their ministries.

PUNAM BENT

Rev. Punam Bent is a Minister of the Word in the Uniting Church in Australia and has been an active religious practitioner for twenty-eight years. She was ordained in the United Methodist Church in Western Ohio in 1992 and migrated to Australia in 1995. She has worked with the Uniting Church in Australia since then.

Punam completed a Master of Divinity from United Theological College in Dayton, Ohio in 1992, and then a second master's in ministry from Charles Sturt University in 2011, with a view to working on a Doctor of Ministry. She has served as a congregational minister in two congregations over ten years, one in the US and then Australia, followed by a career in school chaplaincy for seventeen years.

Punam's education and professional background have offered her extensive experience in providing holistic spiritual and pastoral care to various communities, covering a variety of multi-faith representations. Her cultural background has made it possible for her to work within cross-cultural contexts with ease and intention. She is a passionate advocate for social justice in gender equality, climate justice, and human rights relating to Indigenous rights and the protection of refugees. She is currently writing about mentoring and is also researching the impact of social media influencers on youth. As a woman with an Asian/South Asian ethnic background, she is also working on a book reflecting on her experience as a child of a colony.

QIANWEN DENG

Dr. Qianwen Deng has a PhD from mainland China. She and her husband work alongside service pastors Gordon and Susana Lee to look after various ministry areas at Hills Chinese Service at Hillsong Church, Hills Campus. Deng leads the Mandarin and Cantonese interpretation and translation ministry to provide an interpretation service for the congregation during the weekend services and other study materials and worship songs during the week. By working with Hillsong Music, her team has produced various Mandarin albums and EPs of worship songs.

As a higher education practitioner and early career researcher, Qianwen Deng's research interest focuses on educational theories with a postcolonial edge, including post-monolingual higher education, internationalization, and reciprocity in higher education. She is passionate about highlighting Asian voices in higher education and the decolonization of university pedagogy. Her forthcoming book chapter and article include:

> Deng, Qianwen, and M. Gurbachan Singh. "Disrupting Critical Thinking in Research Methods with Shèn Sī Míngbiàn (慎思明辨)." In *Translanguaging in Educational Research through Multilingual, Intercultural Methods*, forthcoming.

> Deng, Qianwen. "One Size Fits All? A Case Study of Post-Monolingual Critical Thinking in Australian Theological Postgraduate Education." Special Issue: *The Spirit's Voice from the Margin: Disentangling Australasian Pentecostalism from White Hegemony. Australasian Pentecostal Studies* 22, no. 2 (Nov 2021).

APPENDIX 1

RADHIKA SUKUMAR-WHITE

Rev. Radhika Sukumar-White has been a Minister of the Word in the Uniting Church in Australia since 2016. She is a second-generation Sri Lankan Tamil Australian and grew up in Canberra before moving to Sydney to study physiotherapy, music, and then theology. Radhika is passionate about leading dynamic and sacred worship, preaching and teaching, and walking alongside individuals in their life and faith journeys. Radhika currently serves as Ministry Team Leader at Leichhardt Uniting Church, a young, vibrant, affirming, justice-oriented community of faith in the Inner West of Sydney. She serves alongside her husband, who also serves as Chaplain at the University of Sydney. Radhika is also passionate about brunch. Here are two examples of her writing:

- https://uniting.church/towards-intentionally-anti-racist-worship/
- https://www.insights.uca.org.au/leichardt-uniting-church-rallies-to-kill-the-bills/

SANDIE CORNISH

Dr. Sandie Cornish is a practitioner in the field of Catholic Social Teaching. She works with the Office for Social Justice of the Australian Catholic Bishops Conference and is a sessional lecturer with the Australian Catholic University and BBI—TAITE. She is a Member of the Vatican Dicastery for the Promotion of Integral Human Development.

Sandie Cornish has been Director of Quality and Community Engagement for the Sydney College of Divinity, Province Director of Mission of the Society of the Sacred Heart in Australia and New Zealand and has worked with the Good Shepherd Sisters in research and social policy. She has worked with the Australian Jesuits in research, policy, planning, and formation in their social ministries and led the Hong Kong-based Asian Center for the Progress of Peoples.

Sandie Cornish holds a PhD in Practical Theology, a Licentiate in Catholic Social Doctrine and Ethics from the Pontifical

Gregorian University, a Master of Public Policy, and a Bachelor of Economics. Sandie's significant publications include *Still Listening to the Spirit: Woman and Man Twenty Years Later* (Australian Catholic Bishops Conference: Sydney, 2019), which she edited with Andrea Dean; "The Council's Call to Renewed Social Engagement," with Bruce Duncan, in *Vatican II: Reception and Implementation in the Australian Church*, edited by Neil Ormerod et al. (Garratt, 2012); and "Connecting Catholic Social Teaching to Contemporary Australia," with David Freeman, in *Catholic Social Teaching in Global Perspective*, edited by Daniel McDonald S. J. (Orbis, 2010). She has a chapter in the forthcoming Laudato Si' Reader to be published by the Dicastery for the Promotion of Integral Human Development.

SARAH DO

Sarah Do has completed a Master of Divinity with the University of Divinity, having written a minor thesis on Philippians. She is passionate about supporting CALD/LOTE students in their theological studies at Whitley College. She also serves at her local Vietnamese church community, contributing to the Children's Ministry and worship.

Sarah Do's forthcoming publication is "Good Work, Missio Dei, and a Gospel-Worthy Life in Philippians," in *Refaithing Work: Theological and Missiological Perspectives for a Disrupted Age*, edited by Darren Cronshaw, Margaret Kappelhoff, and Steve Taylor (Leiden: Brill, 2022).

THRESI MAUBOY WOHANGARA

Rev. Thresi Mauboy Wohangara is an Indonesian woman who grew up in West Timor. She studied a Bachelor of Theology at ARTHA WACANA Christian University in West Timor. She was ordained as a Minister of the Word twenty-nine years ago in the Evangelical Protestant Church in Timor (GMIT). In 1995, she moved to Australia. She assisted the minister in the congregation in sacrament and then became the full-time minister. Then in 2005, the

APPENDIX 1

Uniting Church of Australia (UCA) recognized her as a minister within UCA. She has served congregations in both Indonesia and Australia. She was the first female Chairperson for the Indonesian National Conference of Uniting Church in Australia and consulted the Asian Manager for Uniting World with the partner church in Asia. She was also part of the National Multicultural Reference Committee. She is currently the Moderator of the Northern Synod of the Uniting Church in Australia.

Thresi is a strong woman of faith and prayer, recognizing that her call to ministry is a call from God. Her motto: "I don't pray for an opportunity but pray that I will be ready when the opportunity comes." She acknowledges the movement of the Holy Spirit in every part of her life.

XIAOLI YANG

Dr. Xiaoli Yang was raised in various subcultures of Asia and moved to Australia as an overseas student at university. She was involved in pioneering and pastoring a multilingual Asian church within a megachurch for seven years following her professional accounting career. Since 2007, Xiaoli has been teaching and equipping leaders locally and abroad in academic and church settings. She is an ordained minister, an accredited spiritual director, and a bilingual poet.

Xiaoli Yang's PhD from the University of Divinity offers a conversation between the Chinese soul-searching and the gospel of Jesus Christ through a unique contextual poetic lens (Leiden: Brill, 2018). So far, she has published nearly two dozen academic writings on intercultural theology. Her poetry has been published and used in spiritual direction and retreats. Amongst other projects, she is working on a Bible commentary on John's letters from Asian perspectives and a book on a theology of migration. She serves on the Australian Association of Mission Studies executive committee and the editorial board of the *Australian Journal of Mission Studies*. She is also a convener of Chinese Missiology in the International Association of Mission Studies. She is fluent in Mandarin, Cantonese, and several other dialects.

Appendix 2

18 Asian and Asian Diaspora Women Theologians You Should Know

Asian female theologians write some of the most creative and vital theology today. These Asian female theologians live in Asia and among the diaspora (in North America, Europe, Australia, etc.). Many of them do classic and contextual theological work. But they are also often practitioner-theologians, pastor-theologians, or activist-theologians.

Asian females make up at least 30 percent of the world's population (and even more when you include those living outside of Asia). But when you ask pastors, theological students, or even theologians to name Asian female theologians, they are often at a loss. Many can't name any (or, at best, they can name only a few).

But the global movement of Asian women doing theology is growing and diverse. And it is becoming increasingly prominent and influential. Kwok Pui-Lan talks about the diversity and importance of Asian female theologians this way:

> More than half of the world's population live in Asia, a multicultural and multireligious continent that has undergone tremendous transformation during the past several decades. From Japan to Indonesia, and from the Philippines to Central Asia, people live in different socio-political realities and divergent cultural worlds. Divided into at least seven linguistic zones, Asia is

Appendix 2

also the birthplace of the major historical religions of humankind.[1]

Kwok Pui-Lan goes on to say, "Asian women comprise more than a quarter of the world's population. They live on a fascinating multilingual, multireligious, and multiracial continent" and in diaspora all over the world. Asian cultures have "diverse eating habits, ways of life, and social and cultural realities." Asian female theological voices are shaped by "immense cultural and religious diversity" and are "pluralistic and multivocal, woven out of many separate strands."[2]

As we learn from Asian female theologians, it is essential to remember that their voices are diverse and many. As Rita Nakashima Brock says, "We differ as much from each other in culture and language as we do from white, Eurocentric feminism," or from white male authors.

Unfortunately, the ignorance about Asian female theologians and their writings is widespread and persistent. It is due time for this to change. The local and global church needs the voices and contributions of Asian women. These Asian female voices enrich our theology, revitalize our churches, and renew the world.

For this reason, we feature eighteen Asian female theologians you should know. We have chosen these eighteen because they have been influential in our personal lives and how we think about and practice our faith and theology. And at the end of the article, we offer 114 more Asian female theologians whose work we are growing to admire and enjoy.

You can access our post "18 Asian Female Theologians You Should Know About (Plus Others for You to Explore)" at these online locations:

- https://theglobalchurchproject.com/18-asian-female-theologians/
- https://grahamjosephhill.com/18-asian-female-theologians/

---

1. Pui-Lan, *Introducing Asian Feminist Theology*, 9. In this quote, Pui-Lan is referring specifically to Asian feminist theologians and their plurality, diversity, and large number.

2. Pui-Lan, *Introducing Asian Feminist Theology*, 9–12.

Appendix 3

Women Theologians of Global Christianity

SERIES EDITOR: GRAHAM JOSEPH HILL

Article Authors in the Series: Jocabed Solano, Drew Jennings-Grisham, Stephanie A. Lowery, Emmanuella Carter, Juliany González Nieves, Grace Al-Zoughbi Arteen, Jessie Giyou Kim, Jen Barker, and Celucien L. Joseph.

In my book *Global Church*, I outlined how Majority World, diaspora, and Indigenous churches and theologies redefine twenty-first century Christianity. Women of color lead much of this new theology and vitality.

Those of us in the West need a new narrative.[1] It's time to abandon our flawed Eurocentric, Americentric, androcentric worldviews. It's past time we expanded our theologies, which are often characterized by the same emphases. We need diverse voices and a new and global narrative. We must turn to the churches and theologies of Majority World, Indigenous, and diaspora (immigrant) cultures (including Asian Australian and Asian American voices). They can help us explore what it means to be a global, vibrant, witnessing community. Many Christian communities in Majority World and Indigenous contexts have been wrestling with

1. Hill, *Global Church*, 13–20 and 415–49.

these issues for generations. Marginalization, persecution, and alienation have been their lot. Yet, somehow, in spite or because of that, they've flourished and grown exponentially.

The quality and quantity of material coming out of the Majority World is astonishing. Any theology that ignores the insights of Indigenous and Majority World Christians is deficient and impoverished. And much of this theological work is being done by women theologians.

White, middle-class, European, North American, tertiary-educated men dominate Western theology and Western theological curriculum and institutions. I know I fit that profile, and I'm calling for change. This group still monopolizes church conferences and seminars, and they are overrepresented as theological faculty and authors. They get most of the book contracts. This group still controls theology and church in many settings. But this is changing. New voices are rising. These include women, minorities, the poor, Indigenous groups, and Majority World leaders. Majority World, diaspora, African American, and Indigenous voices have extraordinary insight and vitality. Openness to other voices needs to happen now. It is time for Western churches, theologies, and missions to mature and reflect God's global church.

It is due time for the global church to hear and honor the voices of women doing theology. We need to listen and learn from African, Asian, Eastern European, Middle Eastern, Caribbean, Latin American, First Nation, diaspora, Indigenous, and Black women theologians. They dare us to examine, decolonize, and reshape our theologies, missions, and churches. And they inspire us to renew the worship, community, and mission of Jesus's church. They stir us to think in fresh ways about what it means to be salt, light, and a city. They help us become a deep and diverse global-local church.

In this series, we profile the work of women theologians of global Christianity. Most of these posts are written by women about women doing theology from their context and culture. We hope that this will inspire you to listen and learn from (and be taught by) the women theologians of global Christianity.

Dr. Gina A. Zurlo, co-director of the Center for the Study of Global Christianity, writes:

Women Theologians of Global Christianity

This series is important for many reasons, including:

- A core part of studying World Christianity is hearing the voices of Christians from around the world. What better way than to learn about the experiences of women from women themselves?

- In general, women historically did not write books and some historians concluded that women did not think theologically. This is completely untrue, and there is a growing body of theological work by women for us to explore.

- Theology courses at Evangelical/conservative seminaries tragically neglect women's voices and generally don't assign books written by women. These lists can provide a helpful corrective.

- These lists remove the frequent excuse used by many male Christian leaders, "But I just don't know any women to ask" when considering guest speakers, lecturers, and commentators. Now you do.

- Reading women's theology from around the world helps us understand on a deeper level the experiences, struggles, and joys of Christian women. Knowing their stories and thoughts helps knit us together as a global Christian family.

- Women are speaking and teaching, and it is our job to sit and listen.

I want to encourage readers to check out the works of these women and expand your horizons. Even if you come from a tradition that does not include women in all leadership roles in the church, or you are not convinced yourself, be open to having your faith expanded and challenged by the voices of women from around the world.[2]

---

2. Center for the Study of Global Christianity, "Women Theologians You Should Know."

APPENDIX 3

POSTS IN THIS SERIES ON WOMEN THEOLOGIANS OF GLOBAL CHRISTIANITY

We provide the links to all these posts on women theologians of global Christianity here: https://grahamjosephhill.com/women-theologians/.

- Emmanuella Carter, "17 African American Women Theologians You Should Know About"
- Grace Al-Zoughbi Arteen and Graham Joseph Hill, "18 Arab Female Theologians and Christian Leaders You Should Know About"
- Jen Barker and Graham Joseph Hill, "160+ Australian and New Zealander Women in Theology You Should Know About"
- Jen Barker and Graham Joseph Hill, "20 Australian and New Zealander Female Theologians You Should Get to Know in 2020"
- Jessie Giyou Kim and Graham Joseph Hill, "12 Women on Changing the World: A 12-Session Film Series on Transforming Society and Neighborhoods"
- Jessie Giyou Kim and Graham Joseph Hill, "18 Asian Female Theologians You Should Know About (Plus Others for You to Explore)"
- Jocabed Solano and Drew Jennings-Grisham, "Some Indigenous Women Theologians You Should Know About"
- Juliany González Nieves, "23 Latin American Women and USA Latinas in Theology and Religion You Should Know About"
- Stephanie A. Lowery, "9 African Women Theologians You Should Know About"

Additional Posts

- Celucien L. Joseph, "20 Haitian Theologians and Biblical Scholars You Should Know About"
- Juliany González Nieves, "Caribbean Christian Theology: A Bibliography"

AN OPEN INVITATION

If you are a woman and would like to write a post about women doing theology from your culture or context, you are welcome to do so! Please get in touch with Graham Joseph Hill at www.grahamjosephhill.com.

Appendix 4

Questions Used in the Surveys and In-Depth Interviews

1. In which country do you live?
2. Are you female?
3. What is your ethnicity?
4. What is your nationality?
5. What is your country of birth?
6. Are you mainly involved in local service and ministry (in your community or neighborhood) or overseas missions (now or in the past)?
7. What was your parent's reaction about you serving in local ministry or overseas missions?—On a scale from 1 (unsupportive) to 5 (very supportive)
8. Why do you think your parents felt this way?
9. Are your parents Christian?
10. Did your parents determine/guide your decision about where you served and your organization?
11. What were your church's and supporters' reactions to you serving in local ministry or overseas missions?—On a scale from 1 (unsupportive) to 5 (very supportive)
12. Did an ethnic church in Australia primarily send you out?
13. Did they determine/guide your decision about where you served and your organization?

Questions Used in the Surveys and In-Depth Interviews

14. What were your church's or mission agency's reactions to you serving in ministry or missions?—On a scale from 1 (unsupportive) to 5 (very supportive)
15. Did your church community or mission agency determine/guide your decision about where you served?
16. Were your race and gender a factor in how you chose your ministry or mission agency?—On a scale from 1 (not at all) to 5 (definitely)
17. Were your race and gender a factor in how you chose your location to serve?—On a scale from 1 (not at all) to 5 (definitely)
18. Were you given opportunities to serve in ministry or mission?—On a scale from 1 (limited) to 5 (extensive)
19. Were you given a choice in where/how you served?
20. Were your choices where you ended up and for how long?
21. What denomination or theological tradition was/is your institution or church a part of?
22. Are/were you paid less than your male counterparts?
23. Are/were you paid less than your majority culture counterparts?
24. If you were excluded from leadership roles, how would you explain this?
25. Did you experience racism or discrimination in local ministry or overseas missions?—On a scale from 1 (never) to 5 (constant)
26. Did you experience sexism in local ministry or overseas missions?—On a scale from 1 (never) to 5 (constant)
27. Did you experience stereotypes of Asian women in organizations involved in local ministry or global missions?—On a scale from 1 (never) to 5 (constant)
28. What were these stereotypes?
29. Have you experienced more racism in local ministry or overseas missions?
30. Have you experienced more sexism in local ministry or overseas missions?
31. Did this racism, sexism, or discrimination occur within your organization?

Appendix 4

32. Did this racism, sexism, or discrimination occur within leadership?
33. Did this racism, sexism, or discrimination occur within the local church?
34. Did this racism, sexism, or discrimination occur within the local community?
35. If yes to any of these questions on racism, sexism, or discrimination, what impact did this have on you?
36. What limitations and challenges are there in being an Asian Australian woman in ministry and service and missions?—On a scale from 1 (none) to 5 (everything)
37. Tick areas of difficulty on the field (in either local ministry in your church or neighborhood or global mission overseas). Mark all that apply.
    a. The expectation of filling roles that are not my gift
    b. Not being able to use gifts of teaching/preaching
    c. Stand out as different
38. If you have done both local ministries in your church or neighborhood and overseas mission, which setting posed the most sexism, racism, and discrimination?
39. Do you feel the main obstacle is your gender or your race?
40. Have these limitations changed over your time in your country and ministry?
41. Are there benefits and strengths in being an Asian Australian woman in local ministry or global missions?—On a scale from 1 (few) to 5 (abundant)
42. Tick areas of benefits on the local ministry or global mission field. Mark all that apply.
    a. Acceptance within society
    b. Ability to connect with a variety of cultures
    c. Ability to work alongside a specific group that interests you
    d. Opportunities in leadership
43. Have these benefits changed over your time in your country and ministry?
44. In your experience, are Asian Australian women neglected in the study of missions (local or global)? Why or why not?

Questions Used in the Surveys and In-Depth Interviews

45. In your experience, are Asian Australian women neglected when churches choose leaders for ministry? Why or why not?
46. What theological, missiological, sociological, racial, or gendered themes create problems for women in ministry and mission with Asian ethnic backgrounds?
47. What roles do Asian Australian women play in ministry and mission?
48. In your experience, what are the attitudes of Asian Australian women to mission, service, evangelism, welfare, and social justice (acknowledging that this is a large and diverse group)?
49. What have been your experiences of inequality, power, vulnerability, and woundedness in mission (local or overseas mission) or ministry?
50. How did that make you feel, and/or how did you respond?
51. What have you heard about the experiences of inequality, power, vulnerability, and woundedness among other Asian Australian women in missions (local or overseas missions) or in local church ministry?
52. How did that make you feel, and/or how did you respond?
53. How is the church's mission enhanced by releasing Asian Australian women to local and overseas missions?
54. How is the church's ministry enhanced by releasing Asian Australian women to local church ministry?
55. What are your suggestions about how the church can deal with the inequalities, racism, or sexism we have discussed?
56. What are your suggestions about how the church can honor and release women with an Asian ethnic background to local ministry and/or overseas missions?
57. Would you like to share any experiences when you may have experienced inequality, power, vulnerability while serving in ministry or missions?
58. Is there anything else you would like to say on these issues?
59. Do you permit us to use your responses (in a de-identified way)?
60. Do you permit us to quote any of your responses (in a de-identified way)?[1]

---

1. University of Divinity HREC approval reference number 371/20.

Authors and Contributors

GRAHAM JOSEPH HILL—AUTHOR

Graham Joseph Hill is Principal of Stirling Theological College and Associate Professor of Global Christianity at the University of Divinity, Australia. His author website is grahamjosephhill.com. Graham has planted and pastored churches and been in theological education for over twenty years. Graham earned a PhD in theology through Flinders University, Australia. He is the author or editor of eleven books including, *Holding Up Half the Sky*, *Hide This in Your Heart* (co-authored with Michael Frost), *Global Church*, *Healing Our Broken Humanity* (co-authored with Grace Ji-Sun Kim), and *Salt, Light, and a City* (two volumes). Graham also directs TheGlobalChurchProject.com.

JESSIE GIYOU KIM—RESEARCH SUPPORT

Jessie Giyou Kim graduated with a Bachelor of Theology through the Australian College of Theology. She serves in ministry at a Baptist Church in Sydney. Jessie was born in Seoul, South Korea, and moved to China at age fifteen. Jessie has served in missions in China, Australia, Cambodia, and Vietnam. Her areas of interest include mission, children's ministry, and caring for people. She is pursuing ordination for pastoral ministry with the Baptist Churches of Australia to become a pastor and missionary. Jessie grew up in various parts of Asia and is fluent in Chinese, Korean, and English. Jessie Giyou Kim supported research for this book

AUTHORS AND CONTRIBUTORS

and TheGlobalChurchProject.com by researching Asian and Asian diaspora theologians and translating publications into Chinese and Korean.

GRACE LUNG—FOREWORD

Grace Lung's passion is restoring brokenness in cultural communities to Jesus through contextualizing the gospel to Asian Australians and developing Asian churches in Australia. Grace is a graduate of Sydney Missionary and Bible College and Fuller Theological Seminary and is currently doing postgraduate studies through Stirling Theological College.

Grace Lung was an Anglican Deaconess Ministries Summer Fellow in 2019. Her writing has appeared in SOLA Network, the Gospel Coalition Australia, Ethos (EA Centre for Christianity and Society), and Centered: Resources for the Asian American Church. In her current roles, she serves on the pastoral staff at Brisbane Chinese Alliance Church, works with the Centre of Asian Christianity at the Brisbane School of Theology, hosts a podcast "Did You Eat Yet?" with the RICE Movement, and serves on OMF Australia Queensland's Ministry Team. Grace has produced the *Asians Between Cultures* course, which helps faith leaders in Asian contexts discover how understanding the gospel with both ethnicity and faith can transform their ministry and relationships. Her website is gracelung.com.

HANNA HYUN—FOREWORD

Hanna Hyun studies Muslim diasporas settled in pluralistic communities, mainly in the United States and Australia. She completed her PhD in Intercultural Studies at the Reformed Theological Seminary in Jackson, Mississippi, in the United States, and served as an assistant professor at Kosin University, South Korea, between 2013 and 2015. Hanna worked at the Sydney College of Divinity from 2016 to 2020. She currently serves as an adjunct professor at Juan International University, South Korea, and has served as director of the Centre for Islamic Studies in Sydney, Australia, since 2018. Her main research areas are Islamic studies, migration and diaspora theology, refugee and asylum seeker studies, multicultural church planting, and women in mission.

GRACE JI-SUN KIM—AFTERWORD

Grace Ji-Sun Kim is Professor of Theology at Earlham School of Religion. Englewood Review of Books listed *Intersectional Theology* (co-written with Susan Shaw) as one of the Best Theology Books of 2018. *Healing Our Broken Humanity* (co-written with Graham Hill) was included in Englewood Review of Books list of Best Books of 2018. Grace Ji-Sun Kim is a member of the Board of Directors for the American Academy of Religion. She served on the American Academy of Religion's (AAR) "Research Grants Jury Committee" and was co-chair of AAR's steering committee, "Women of Color Scholarship, Teaching and Activism Group." She sits on the editorial board for the *Journal for Religion and Popular Culture* and is a referee for three journals, including the *Journal of Race, Ethnicity, and Religion*. She is an Advisory Board Member for the Center for Reconciliation at Duke Divinity School.[2] Grace Ji-Sun Kim is the author or editor of twenty books. Grace hosts the Madang podcast and blogs at gracejisunkim.wordpress.com.

---

2. Grace Ji-Sun Kim's website: https://gracejisunkim.wordpress.com/about/.

More Books by Graham Joseph Hill

Graham Joseph Hill and Desiree Geldenhuys. *The Soul Online: Bereavement, Social Media, and Competent Care.* Eugene, OR: Cascade, 2021.

Graham Joseph Hill. *Salt, Light, and a City: Ecclesiology for the Global Missional Community: Volume 2, Majority World Voices.* Eugene, OR: Cascade, 2020.

Graham Joseph Hill and Michael Frost. *Hide This in Your Heart: The Bible for Radicals and Activists.* Colorado Springs, CO, 2020.

Graham Joseph Hill, ed. *Relentless Love: Living Out Integral Mission to Combat Poverty, Injustice and Conflict.* Carlisle, Cumbria: Micah Global and Langham, 2020.

Graham Joseph Hill. *Holding Up Half the Sky: A Biblical Case for Women Leading and Teaching in the Church.* Eugene, OR: Cascade, 2020.

Graham Joseph Hill and Grace Ji-Sun Kim. *Healing our Broken Humanity: Practices for Revitalizing the Church and Renewing the World.* Downers Grove, IL: IVP, 2018.

More Books by Graham Joseph Hill

Graham Joseph Hill. *Salt, Light, and a City: Ecclesiology for the Global Missional Community: Volume 1, Western Voices.* 2nd ed. Eugene, OR: Cascade, 2017.

Graham Joseph Hill. *GlobalChurch: Reshaping Our Conversations, Renewing Our Mission, Revitalizing Our Churches.* Downers Grove, IL: IVP Academic, 2016.

Graham Joseph Hill, ed. *Signs of Hope in the City: Renewing Urban Mission, Embracing Radical Hope.* Melbourne: International Society for Urban Mission, 2015.

Graham Joseph Hill, ed. *Servantship: Sixteen Servants on the Four Movements of Radical Servantship.* Eugene, OR: Wipf and Stock, 2013.

Graham Joseph Hill. *Salt, Light, and a City: Introducing Missional Ecclesiology.* Eugene, OR: Wipf and Stock, 2012.

Bibliography

ACSPRI. "The Australian Survey of Social Attitudes (Aussa)." Accessed July 9, 2021. https://www.acspri.org.au/aussa.
Allen, Suzanne. "Creative Diversity: Promoting Interculturality in Australian Pathways to Higher Education." *Journal of International Students* 8, no. 1 (January 1, 2018) 251.
Anderson, Robert J., and William A. Adams. *Scaling Leadership: Building Organizational Capability and Capacity to Create Outcomes That Matter Most.* New York, NY: John Wiley and Sons, 2019.
Australian Bureau of Statistics. "Migration, Australia." Accessed July 8, 2021. https://www.abs.gov.au/statistics/people/population/migration-australia.
Australian Bureau of Statistics. "Migration, Australia: Statistics on Australia's International Migration, Internal Migration (Interstate and Intrastate), and the Population by Country of Birth." Accessed July 8, 2021. https://www.abs.gov.au/statistics/people/population/migration-australia/latest-release.
Australians Together. "Indigenous Disadvantage in Australia: The Disparity between Indigenous and Non-Indigenous Australians." Accessed July 19, 2021. https://australianstogether.org.au/discover/the-wound/indigenous-disadvantage-in-australia/.
Baird, Julia. *Media Tarts: How the Australian Press Frames Female Politicians.* Melbourne: Scribe, 2004.
———. "What's Changed 17 Years after I Wrote a Book About the Media, Women and Politics." *Sydney Morning Herald*, July 24, 2021. https://www.smh.com.au/national/what-s-changed-17-years-after-i-wrote-a-book-about-the-media-women-and-politics-20210723-p58cbc.html.
Beeghly, Erin. "What's Wrong with Stereotypes? The Falsity Hypothesis." *Social Theory and Practice* 47, no. 1 (January 2021) 33–61.

Bibliography

Bevans, Stephen B., et al.. "Missiology after Bosch: Reverencing a Classic by Moving Beyond." *International Bulletin of Missionary Research* 29, no. 2 (2005) 69–72.

Carole, Ferrier. "Preoccupations of Some Asian Australian Women's Fiction at the Turn of the Twenty-First Century." *eTropic: Electronic Journal of Studies in the Tropics* 16, no. 2 (January 12, 2017). http://dx.doi.org/10.25120/etropic.20.1.2021.3768.

Carter, J. Kameron. *Race: A Theological Account.* Oxford: Oxford University Press, 2008.

Center for the Study of Global Christianity. "Women Theologians You Should Know About from the Global Church Project." Gordon Conwell Theological Seminary, 2021. Accessed July 24, 2021. https://www.gordonconwell.edu/blog/women-theologians-you-should-know-about-from-the-global-church-project/.

Cho, Eugene. "My Quasi-Conversation with Rob Bell ... About Women." *Eugene Cho: One Day's Wages*, April 16, 2008. https://eugenecho.com/2008/04/16/my-conversation-with-rob-bell/.

Clark, Juliet. "Perceptions of Australian Cultural Identity among Asian Australians." *Australian Journal of Social Issues* 42, no. 3 (March 22, 2007) 303.

Collins, Patricia Hill. "Intersectionality's Definitional Dilemmas." *Annual Review of Sociology* 41 (2015) 1–20.

Common Grace. "Aboriginal and Torres Strait Islander Justice." Accessed July 19, 2021. https://www.commongrace.org.au/aboriginal_and_torres_strait_islander_justice.

Crenshaw, Kimberlé Williams. "Mapping the Margins: Intersectionality, Identity Politics, and Violence against Women of Color." *Stanford Law Review* 43, no. 6 (1991) 1241–99.

Crumm, David, "Diana Butler Bass: 'We Cannot Stand By ...'" *Read the Spirit: David Crumm Media*, October 16, 2016. https://readthespirit.com/explore/diana-butler-bass-we-cannot-stand-by/.

Cruz, Gemma Tulud. *An Intercultural Theology of Migration: Pilgrims in the Wilderness.* Studies in Systematic Theology. Leiden: Brill, 2010.

———. *Toward a Theology of Migration: Social Justice and Religious Experience.* Content and Context in Theological Ethics. New York, NY: Palgrave Macmillan, 2014.

Davis, Angela Y. *Women, Race and Class.* New York: Vintage, 1983.

DeBorst, Ruth Padilla. "'Unexpected' Guests at God's Banquet Table: Gospel in Mission and Culture." *Evangelical Review of Theology* 33, no. 1 (2009) 62–76.

Elias, Amanuel, et al. *Racism in Australia Today.* Melbourne: Palgrave Macmillan, 2021.

Emerson, Michael O., and Christian Smith. *Divided by Faith: Evangelical Religion and the Problem of Race in America.* Oxford: Oxford University Press, 2000.

BIBLIOGRAPHY

Equality Rights Alliance. "Gender Equality in Australia." Accessed July 19, 2021. https://www.equalityrightsalliance.org.au/who-we-are/gender-equality-in-australia/.

Evans, Rachel Held. "'More Than Serving Tea': A Conversation with Kathy Khang and Nikki Toyama-Szeto." July 19, 2013. https://rachelheldevans.com/blog/more-than-serving-tea.

Finger, Reta Halteman. *Of Widows and Meals: Communal Meals in the Book of Acts*. Grand Rapids, MI: Eerdmans, 2007.

Grant, Stan. *Australia Day*. Sydney: HarperCollins, 2019.

——. "The Australian Dream: Blood, History and Becoming." *Quarterly Essay* 64 (November 21, 2016).

——. *Talking to My Country*. Sydney: HarperCollins, 2016.

Haslanger, Sally. "Race, Intersectionality, and Method: A Reply to Critics." *Philosophical Studies* 171 (October 1, 2014) 109–19. https://doi.org/10.1007/s11098-013-0244-1.

——. *Resisting Reality: Social Construction and Social Critique*. New York: Oxford University Press, 2012.

Hatzaw Ciin Sian, Siam. "Reading Esther as a Postcolonial Feminist Icon for Asian Women in Diaspora." *Open Theology* 7, no. 1 (January 1, 2021) 1–34.

Hesse, Monica. "'It's Race, Class and Gender Together': Why the Atlanta Killings Aren't Just About One Thing." *Washington Post*, March 18, 2021. https://www.washingtonpost.com/lifestyle/style/hesse-atlanta-asian-women/2021/03/18/183b3f00-8749-11eb-8a8b-5cf82c3dffe4_story.html.

Hill, Graham Joseph. "4 Qualities of Missional Movements Born at the Margins." *The Global Church Project*, July 14, 2016. https://theglobalchurchproject.com/4-qualities-missional-movements-born-margins/.

——. *Global Church: Reshaping Our Conversations, Renewing Our Mission, Revitalizing Our Churches*. Downers Grove, IL: IVP Academic, 2016.

——. "Hearing and Responding to the Margins." *Common Grace*, July 14, 2016. https://www.commongrace.org.au/the_margins.

——. *Holding Up Half the Sky: A Biblical Case for Women Leading and Teaching in the Church*. Eugene, OR: Cascade, 2020.

——. "Let's Stop Talking About Masculinity and Start Talking About Discipleship." Accessed July 23, 2021. https://www.cbeinternational.org/resource/article/mutuality-blog-magazine/lets-stop-talking-about-masculinity-and-start-talking.

——. *Salt, Light, and a City: Conformation—Ecclesiology for the Global Missional Community: Volume 2, Majority World Voices*. Eugene, OR: Cascade, 2019.

——. "Women Are the Heartbeat of Living Faith." *The Global Church Project*, July 21, 2016. https://theglobalchurchproject.com/women-heartbeat-living-faith/.

Hill, Graham Joseph, and Grace Ji-Sun Kim. *Healing Our Broken Humanity: Practices for Revitalizing the Church and Renewing the World*. Downers Grove, IL: InterVarsity, 2018.

Bibliography

Hollinsworth, David. *Race and Racism in Australia.* 3rd ed. South Melbourne: Thomson, 2006.

Holroyd, Jules, et al. "Responsibility for Implicit Bias." *Philosophy Compass* 12, no. 3 (2017). https://philpapers.org/go.pl?id=HOLRFI-3&proxyId=&u=https%3A%2F%2Fdx.doi.org%2F10.1111%2Fphc3.12410.

Hooper, Chloe. *The Tall Man.* Camberwell: Hamish Hamilton, 2008.

Houston, Lesley. "Marginality, Liminality and a Third Space." Paper presented at ANZATS 2021 Conference: Theological Ethics, Online/Blended Conference, ANZATS, 2021.

Hunter, James Davison. *Culture Wars: The Struggle to Define America.* New York, NY: Basic, 1991.

Jennings, Willie James. *The Christian Imagination: Theology and the Origins of Race.* New Haven, CT: Yale University Press, 2010.

Jihye Chun, Jennifer, et al. "Intersectionality as a Social Movement Strategy: Asian Immigrant Women Advocates." *Intersectionality: Theorizing Power, Empowering Theory* 38, no. 4 (January 1, 2013) 917–40.

Johnson, Elizabeth A. *The Strength of Her Witness: Jesus Christ in the Global Voices of Women.* Maryknoll, NY: Orbis, 2016.

Johnson, Todd M., and Gina A. Zurlo. *World Christian Encyclopedia.* 3rd ed. Edinburgh: Edinburgh University Press, 2020.

Jones, Karen. "Intersectionality and Ameliorative Analyses of Race and Gender." *Philosophical Studies: An International Journal for Philosophy in the Analytic Tradition* 171, no. 1 (October 1, 2014) 99–107.

Jones, Robert P. *The End of White Christian America.* New York, NY: Simon & Schuster, 2016.

Jozuka, Emiko. "Aboriginal Australians Are Earth's Oldest Civilization: DNA Study." *CNN*, September 22, 2016. Accessed July 8, 2021. https://edition.cnn.com/2016/09/22/asia/indigenous-australians-earths-oldest-civilization/.

Kassam, Natasha, and Jennifer Hsu. *Being Chinese in Australia: Public Opinion in Chinese Communities.* Sydney: Lowry Institute, 2021. https://interactives.lowyinstitute.org/features/chinese-communities.

Keum, Brian TaeHyuk, et al. "Gendered Racial Microaggressions Scale for Asian American Women: Development and Initial Validation." *Journal of Counseling Psychology* 65, no. 5 (2018) 571–85.

Khoo, Tseen-Ling. *Banana Bending: Asian-Australian and Asian-Canadian Literatures.* Hong Kong: Hong Kong University Press, 2003.

Kim, Christina L., et al. "Asian and Female in the White God's World: A Qualitative Exploration of Discrimination in Christian Academia." *Mental Health, Religion & Culture* 13, no. 5 (July 2010) 453–65.

Kim, Grace Ji-Sun, and Susan M. Shaw. *Intersectional Theology: An Introductory Guide.* Minneapolis, MN: Fortress, 2018.

Kim, Hyein Amber. "Understanding 'Koreanness': Racial Stratification and Colorism in Korea and Implications for Korean Multicultural Education."

Bibliography

International Journal of Multicultural Education 22, no. 1 (January 1, 2020) 76.

Kim, Matthew D., et al. *Finding Our Voice: A Vision for Asian North American Preaching*. Bellingham, WA: Lexham, 2020.

Kwai, Isabella. "Young Asian-Australians Carve Out an Identity of Their Own." *New York Times*, June 29, 2017.

Kwok, Pui-Lan. *Introducing Asian Feminist Theology*. Sheffield: Sheffield Academic, 2000.

Kyung, Chung Hyun. *Struggle to Be the Sun Again: Introducing Asian Women's Theology*. Maryknoll, NY: Orbis, 1990.

Lee, Lily Xiao Hong, and Sue Wiles. "Gender in Asian Society and Culture." *Journal of the Oriental Society of Australia* 49 (January 1, 2017) 26–31.

Lee-Park, Sun Ai, and Sang Jung Park. "Woman and Man in Community: An Asian Reflection." *Ecumenical Review* 46, no. 2 (1994) 147–56.

Mackellar, Dorothea. *My Country*. Paddington: Pippa Masson, Estate of Dorothea Mackellar, 1908.

Maddison, Sarah. *The Colonial Fantasy: Why White Australia Can't Solve Black Problems*. Sydney: Allen & Unwin, 2019.

Madva, Alex. "A Plea for Anti-Anti-Individualism: How Oversimple Psychology Misleads Social Policy." *Ergo* 3 (2016). Accessed July 8, 2021. https://quod.lib.umich.edu/e/ergo/12405314.0003.027/—plea-for-anti-anti-individualism-how-oversimple-psychology?rgn=main;view=fulltext.

Markus, Andrew. *Mapping Social Cohesion: The Scanlon Foundation Surveys*. Scanlon Foundation. Melbourne: Monash University, 2021. https://scanloninstitute.org.au/sites/default/files/2021-02/SC2020%20Report%20Final.pdf.

Markwick, Alison, et al. "Experiences of Racism among Aboriginal and Torres Strait Islander Adults Living in the Australian State of Victoria: A Cross-Sectional Population-Based Study." *BMC Public Health* 19 (2019) 309. https://doi.org/https://doi.org/10.1186/s12889-019-6614-7. https://bmcpublichealth.biomedcentral.com/articles/10.1186/s12889-019-6614-7.

Massari, Paul, "Racism On Her Mind: Cultural Psychologist Qi Wang Discusses Anti-Asian Stereotypes, Their Impact, and How to Address Them." *Harvard University Graduate School of Arts and Sciences*, May 6, 2021. https://gsas.harvard.edu/news/stories/racism-her-mind.

Matthews, Julie. "Racialised Schooling, 'Ethnic Success' and Asian–Australian Students." *British Journal of Sociology of Education* 23, no. 2 (June 2002) 193–207.

Mayor, Thomas. *Finding the Heart of the Nation: The Journey of the Uluru Statement Towards Voice, Treaty and Truth*. Richmond: Hardie, 2019.

Mazumdar, Sucheta. "Beyond Bound Feet: Relocating Asian American Women." *OAH Magazine of History* 10, no. 4 (January 1, 1996) 23–27.

McCrindle Research. "Australia Then and Now: 30 Years of Change." Accessed July 20, 2021. https://mccrindle.com.au/insights/blogarchive/australia-then-and-now-30-years-of-change/.

BIBLIOGRAPHY

McKnight, Scot. *A Fellowship of Differents: Showing the World God's Design for Life Together.* Grand Rapids, MI: Zondervan, 2015.

Orevillo-Montenegro, Muriel. *The Jesus of Asian Women. Women from the Margins.* Maryknoll, NY: Orbis, 2006.

Orme, Laura M. Northrop, et al. "Power, Sexism, and Gender: Factors in Biblical Interpretation." *Journal of Psychology and Theology* 45, no. 4 (Winter 2017) 274–85.

Park, Sun Ai Lee, and Virginia Fabella. *We Dare to Dream: Doing Theology as Asian Women.* Horizons. Ossining, NY: Orbis, 1990.

Patel, Vaishali, and Margaret Smith Crocco. "Teaching About South Asian Women: Getting Beyond the Stereotypes (Women of the World)." *Social Education* 67, no. 1 (January 1, 2003) 22.

Pattel-Gray, Anne. *The Great White Flood: Racism in Australia; Critically Appraised from an Aboriginal Historico-Theological Viewpoint.* American Academy of Religion Cultural Criticism Series. Atlanta, GA: Scholars, 1998.

Payne, Kaley. "The Future of the Church Is Asian." *Eternity News*, April 4, 2019. Accessed July 19, 2021. https://www.eternitynews.com.au/in-depth/the-future-of-the-church-is-asian/.

Phan, Peter C. "Deus Migrator—God the Migrant: Migration of Theology and Theology of Migration." *Theological Studies* 77, no. 4 (November 17, 2016) 845–68.

Project Implicit. "Project Implicit." Accessed July 8, 2021. https://www.projectimplicit.net/.

Powell, R., et al. *Research Profile 2020.01: National and Protestant Church Attenders Comparison.* Sydney: NCLS, 2020.

———. *Research Profile 2020.02: Asian Female Church Attenders Comparison.* Sydney: NCLS, 2020.

Ramos, Delma, and Varaxy Yi. "Doctoral Women of Color Coping with Racism and Sexism in the Academy." *International Journal of Doctoral Studies* 15, no. 1 (January 1, 2020) 135–45.

Rielly, Derek. *Gulpilil.* Sydney: Pan Macmillan, 2019.

Robinson, Kathryn. "Of Mail-Order Brides and 'Boys' Own' Tales: Representations of Asian-Australian Marriages." *Feminist Review*, no. 52 (March 22, 1996) 53.

Ruether, Rosemary Radford. *To Change the World: Christology and Cultural Criticism.* New York, NY: Crossroad, 1984.

Sadiq, Yousaf. "Jesus' Encounter with a Woman at the Well: A South Asian Perspective." *Missiology* 46, no. 4 (2018) 363–73.

Sayers, Dorothy L. *Are Women Human?* Grand Rapids, MI: Eerdmans, 1971.

Schultz, Julianne, and Sandra Phillips, eds. "First Things First." *Griffith Review* 60. Griffith: Griffith University, 2018.

Schüssler Fiorenza, Elisabeth. *Discipleship of Equals: A Critical Feminist Ekkl[set macron over e]ēsia-Logy of Liberation.* New York, NY: Crossroad, 1993.

BIBLIOGRAPHY

Sechiyama, Kaku. *Patriarchy in East Asia: A Comparative Sociology of Gender.* The Intimate and the Public in Asian and Global Perspectives. Leiden: Brill, 2013.

Tan, Xiao, et al. "Taking the Measure of Prejudice in a Pandemic: Has Covid-19 Heightened Anti-Asian Bias in Australia? A New Survey Shows Some Worrying Signs." *The Interpreter*, March 30, 2021. Accessed July 23, 2021. https://www.lowyinstitute.org/the-interpreter/taking-measure-prejudice-pandemic.

Tang, Flora x. "'Lead Us Not . . .' on Asian Women as Sexual Objects." *America* 224, no. 6 (May 2021) 10.

Tiantian, Zheng, ed. *Cultural Politics of Gender and Sexuality in Contemporary Asia.* Honolulu, HI: University of Hawaii Press, 2016.

Toh, Justine. "'Original Sins' and Racial Justice: What's on the Other Side?" *ABC Religion and Ethics*, July 30, 2020. Accessed July 23, 2021. https://www.abc.net.au/religion/original-sins-and-racial-justice/12509196.

Toyama-Szeto, Nikki, and Tracey Gee. *More Than Serving Tea: Asian American Women on Expectations, Relationships, Leadership and Faith.* Westmont, IL: IVP, 2007.

Tucker, Shirley. "The Great Southern Land: Asian-Australian Women Writers Re-View the Australian Landscape." *Australian Literary Studies* 21, no. 2 (October 1, 2003) 178.

The Uluru Statement. "Uluru Statement from the Heart." Accessed 19 July, 2021. https://ulurustatement.org/.

Western Sydney University. "Face Up to Racism: 2015–16 National Survey." Accessed July 19, 2021. https://www.westernsydney.edu.au/challengingracism/challenging_racism_project/our_research/face_up_to_racism_2015-16_national_survey.

Williams, Blair. "Inside the Toxic Sexist Culture of Australia's Political Bubble." Accessed July 23, 2021. https://www.internationalaffairs.org.au/australianoutlook/inside-the-toxic-sexist-culture-of-australias-political-bubble/.

Winarnita, Monika Swasti. "The Politics and Poetics of Authenticity: Indonesian Migrant Women and Cultural Representation in Perth, Australia." *Journal of the Humanities and Social Sciences of Southeast Asia and Oceania* 171, no. 4 (October 1, 2015) 489.

World Economic Forum. *Global Gender Gap Report 2021.* Geneva: March 2021. https://www.weforum.org/reports/global-gender-gap-report-2021.

Yee, Gale A. "Thinking Intersectionally: Gender, Race, Class, and the Etceteras of Our Discipline." *Journal of Biblical Literature* 139, no. 1 (2020) 7–26.

Zhou, Naaman. "Survey of Covid-19 Racism against Asian Australians Records 178 Incidents in Two Weeks." *The Guardian* (London), April 17, 2020.

www.ingramcontent.com/pod-product-compliance
Lightning Source LLC
Chambersburg PA
CBHW051939160426
43198CB00013B/2220